Radical

Exploring the rise of extremism and
the pathway to peace

Steve Chalke

© Oasis Global
2016

First published in Great Britain in 2016 by Oasis Books,
an Oasis Community Trust brand.

Copyright © Steve Chalke, 2016

A CIP catalogue record for this title is available from the British Library

ISBN: 978-1-910719-17-6

Cover Design by EPLS Design Ltd. Winchester
Typeset in Garamond and Helvetica Neue by EPLS Design Ltd. Winchester

CONTENTS

INTRODUCTION

You can't kill an evil ideology by taking down a person, a thousand people, or even ten thousand people. All you will do is feed it. It will transmute, return and bite you harder.

If we are going to overcome the escalating problem of extremism and terrorism that our world faces, we need a different answer. We need to find a narrative – or group of related narratives – strong enough, compelling enough, infectious enough, deep enough, rooted enough, and radical enough to turn the tide.

The external world of our public actions is inseparably linked to the private world of internal motivation. No solution to our problems with terrorist and extremist behaviour can succeed unless it recognises this link.

If you want to change society, then you have to offer people a more powerful story; a more compelling narrative than the one that they currently serve. Everyone needs a narrative worth living by; one that explains to us who we are, supplies us with a sense of worth and purpose – and which offers us hope for the future. Without this, we are lost.

The problem is that our suggested counter-extremism and counter-terrorism solutions just don't make this connection at the moment. As a result, they fail to get to the heart of things. Instead of tackling the roots – the fundamentals – of the issue, they attempt to deal with the symptoms of its growth. In a phrase, they are just not radical enough.

In the summer of 2015 I began to write a paper on the issues of Islamic extremism and radicalisation as well as those of wider gang culture. It was an internal document for Oasis, the charity that I work for, to act as a stimulus to our discussion about some of the challenges in some of the communities we work in. But one morning whilst out jogging I realised suddenly that it should actually be a book; a book for everyone. And this is it.

'Radical' is written to invite comment, to stimulate conversation, to create debate and to inspire action. It is intended to raise questions for academics and practitioners, for schools and universities, for children's and youth workers, for central and local government, for police and security agencies, for businesses and the media, for the Church and for Islam, for other faith and community groups, for all of us in our everyday lives and relationships.

But before we get started, a couple of important caveats:

Firstly, I have occasionally – for shorthand – talked of Western thinking as opposed to Islamic culture and thought. Although, in broad terms, there are some very important differences that it is essential we grasp, to see the West as a monolith, and the Muslim world as entirely separate to it, is to oversimplify dangerously.

Although we tend to view minorities as homogenous units – it's an easy way of getting a handle on them – Islam is not monolithic. Islamic communities come in as many shades and varieties as churches, dance groups or cheeses. Added to this, there are many Westerners who are Muslims, just as there are many non-westerners who are non-Muslims.

In fact, our identities are always complex. I get called a Westerner, but I want to say 'yes I am' and 'no I'm not'. By birth and upbringing I am Anglo-Indian, both English and Indian. Secondly, I'm a Christian, rather than a disciple of the West's most dominant philosophy – secular humanism. At the same time, however, I find some of the thinking behind the core concepts of Islam really inspirational; for instance, the idea of the Ummah – the traditional emphasis on the oneness or togetherness of the whole community – is deeply attractive to me. Like many others, I mourn the loss of community and belonging, in the West.

So when we use a phrase like *the clash of civilisations* we make a grave error. The West versus Islam language is both problematic and misleading. Demonising *the other* only ever produces heat rather than light, and the situation is just not that binary anyway. The issues are far more nuanced.

Secondly, we can too easily fall into the trap of being divided by the usage of the same language, whilst assuming we all know what we are talking about and that we mean the same thing. The problem is, as we will discover, that in this area, the same language is used by different groups to mean very different things. In fact, that is exactly where a lot of the tension is generated.

Much of the terminology around the issue of Islamic extremism and terrorism is highly politicised and lacks clear definition. So, for instance, the term 'Islamist' finds itself used by some to describe a genuine Islamic faith commitment, and by others – especially politicians, the media, and security forces – to speak of criminals. And, to add even more complexity, the same group can, as I have discovered whilst researching this book, mean different things by the same term in different contexts.

Lastly, none of this is me standing apart from these issues as some kind of detached commentator; I am in the middle of it, searching for answers along with everyone else. These problems have taken a long time in the making and will not be solved overnight. Together, however, I do believe that we can find a narrative – in our shared humanity – that is radical enough to turn the tide.

My thanks to the host of people who have helped me with this manuscript; especially to Yasmeen Akhtar, Arthur Brown, Jim Currell, Keith Dennis, Nancy Doyle, Elaine Dunn, Paul East,

Barrie Evans, Amanda Faul, Howard Green, Kowsar Hoque, Joy Madeiros, Tarek Mohammed, Graham Mungeam, Jill Rowe, Arnie Swiegers, John Whiter and Mohammed Abu Zaid. The wisdom is theirs – any remaining shortcomings are mine.

ONE
The War on Terror

"Our war on terror begins with al-Qaeda, but it does not end there. It will not end until every terrorist group of global reach has been found, stopped and defeated."

It was the evening of September 20th 2001, when George W. Bush uttered these fateful words to Congress in Washington, nine days after members of al-Qaeda's Hamburg cell had launched their infamous attack on America, killing a total of 2,977 people.[1]

The terrorist assault on New York and Washington in September 2001 was a key moment for the world. Tony Blair, then the serving British Prime Minister, was later to describe it as *"the determining moment of my premiership"*, adding, *"On that day and subsequently, I thought the duty of my country was to stand – as I put it – 'shoulder to shoulder' with America."*[2]

Less than a month later, the US and her allies had launched *Operation Enduring Freedom,* invading Afghanistan, demanding that the Taliban expel al-Qaeda, and that they hand over its leader, Osama bin Laden. Initially, the mood in the West was confident. By the time Bush delivered his *2002 State of the Union Address* at the United States Capitol building on January 29th, an interim Afghan government had been formed and he was able to assert, to cheers from his audience:

"The American flag flies again over our embassy in Kabul. Terrorists who once occupied Afghanistan, now occupy cells at Guantanamo Bay."[3]

Fourteen years later, a study by Brown University's, Watson Institute for International Studies, called *Costs of War*, looked at war-related deaths, injuries and displacement in Afghanistan and Pakistan from 2001 to 2014. Since the overthrow of the Taliban regime, it estimates that almost 100,000 people including civilians, children, aid workers, soldiers and militants had been killed in Afghanistan, whilst another 100,000 had been seriously wounded. In neighbouring Pakistan, civilian and military deaths totalled around another 50,000, with a further 60,000 seriously wounded. In both countries many tens of thousands more civilians have faced displacement, all with no lasting resolution in sight.

Noting a rise in annual figures for those killed and wounded in both countries over recent years, Dr Neta Crawford, the academic who headed up the report team, commented that the figures demonstrate that far from the war in Afghanistan coming to an end, *"It is getting worse".*[4]

More than that, over the years since Bush's *'war on terror'* was launched, terror and terrorism have escalated around the world. The second Iraq War – the protracted armed conflict that began with a surprise invasion in 2003 led by the United States and her allies – has not proved to be decisive either.[5] Meanwhile, hundreds of terror attacks by extremist groups – the vast majority of them by Islamic terrorists – have taken place, around the globe, on what is now almost a daily basis, with attackers using a multitude of deadly tactics including arson, bombings, suicide attacks, car bombs, van and lorry bombs, rockets, spree shootings, stabbings, hijackings, kidnappings and beheadings.

During 2015 alone there were a total of 386 separate terrorist attacks in countries as diverse as Afghanistan, Australia, Bahrain, Bangladesh, Bosnia and Herzegovina, Cameroon, Chad, China, Egypt, France, Germany, India, Indonesia, Iraq, Ireland, Israel, Kenya, Kuwait, Lebanon, Libya, Macedonia, Mali, Niger, Nigeria, Pakistan, Philippines, Japan, Russia, Saudi Arabia, Somalia, Sri Lanka, Syria, Thailand, Tunisia, Turkey, Ukraine, United States, the United Kingdom, the West Bank, and Yemen.[6]

The proliferation of groups perpetrating these crimes is also striking. Once again, in 2015, beside 'lone-wolf' operators, groups who have claimed responsibility for terrorist attacks include Boko Haram, Bangsamoro Islamic Freedom Fighters, various Taliban related groups, several branches of al-Qaeda, al-Shabaab, al-Nusra Front, Donetsk People's Republic, Real Irish Republican Army, Abu Sayaf, Moro Islamic Liberation Front, Jundullah, New People's Army, Jamaat-ul-Ahrar, al-Mourabitoun, Baluch Liberation Front, the Wahhabist movement and the Islamic State of Iraq and Syria (ISIS), otherwise known as Islamic State of Iraq and the Levant (ISIL) or simply Daesh.[7] However, as I write, it is now eighteen months since ISIS declared the territories it controls as a single caliphate and renamed itself Islamic State.[8]

Indeed, another 2015 report entitled *'Inside the Jihadi Mind'*, from *The Centre on Religion & Geopolitics*, sponsored by the Blair Foundation, explains that; *'After the 9/11 attacks, Osama bin Laden's al-Qaeda had approximately 300 militants. ISIS alone now has, at a low estimate, 31,000 fighters across Syria and Iraq.'*[9]

Meanwhile, in January 2015, Germany's intelligence chief, Hans-Georg Maaßen, reported that, in his country, the number of Salafists – the ultra-conservative orthodox stream within Sunni Islam, one wing of which has bred al-Qaeda, ISIS and many other terrorist groups – had grown from 3,800 to 6,300 in three years.[10]

Fourteen years on from the terrible events of September 11th 2001, the problem of terrorism is far deeper and broader than the architects of the West's original response ever imagined. It now impacts on countless millions of people across the world who have had their lives completely upturned or damaged by it. What is clearer than ever is that it's time to think differently because if anything about the current situation is for certain, it is that the same old approach will always yield the same old outcomes.

Lifelong learning

An article that appeared in the London Guardian, on September 13th 2001, just a few days after the Twin Towers attack, written by Seumas Milne, makes sobering reading: *'Shock, rage and grief there has been aplenty. But any glimmer of recognition of why people might have been driven to carry out such atrocities, sacrificing their own lives in the process – or why the United States is hated with such bitterness, not only in Arab and Muslim countries, but across the developing world – seems almost entirely absent.'*

Perhaps the words of Bill Schwartz, Archdeacon in the Gulf for the Anglican Diocese of Cyprus and the Gulf, in his book *'Islam: A Religion, A Culture, A Society'*, also offer pause for thought: '... *in the months after 9/11 I was often asked by American friends, "Why do they hate us?" To my amazement, even though the question was asked quite often and with real sincerity, very few of those who asked really showed any interest in pursuing discussion towards exploring that question.'*[11]

What might America, the UK and the other Western allies have learned if we had chosen to stop, listen and reflect in 2001? To bring a voice from the past to that 'never-had' discussion, listen to the words Georges Clemenceau, the French Prime Minister, who played a leading role in the drafting of the Treaty of Versailles, the signing of which brought a formal end to *'the war to end all wars'*, World War I. *"It is easier to make war than make peace,"* he reflected.[12]

The stringent terms imposed by Versailles on Germany, in 1919, were even opposed by many of those who were involved, from all sides, in the drafting process itself. In his book '*The Economic Consequences of the Peace*', the famed economist, John Maynard Keynes, who attended as a delegate of the British Treasury, called the outcome a '*Carthaginian peace*'; a misguided attempt to humiliate and crush Germany further, rather than to follow wiser principles which would have offered more opportunity to build a secure future for all.[13] His verdict was that it amounted to "... *one of the most serious acts of political unwisdom for which our statesmen have ever been responsible.*"

Combined with the political turmoil within Germany and the adverse international economic situation, the Great Depression of the 1930s,[14] the terms of the Versailles settlement were, in time, to create what many regard as a perfect storm. The harshness of the treaty was denounced by Germans of all political shades – particularly what became known as the 'Guilt Clause' which blamed Germany for starting the war – as an insult to the nation's honour.

This legacy was to play a central role in the development of German politics during the 1920s and 1930s. Historians and commentators still argue over whether or not Versailles led inevitably to the outbreak of World War II, and if so which aspect of the settlement did the most damage. Was it the humiliation of the 'Guilt Clause' or the vacuum left by a crushing military campaign without proper thought being given to rebuilding the infrastructure of the defeated nation? Without doubt, the mix of bitter resentment, crippling socio-economic conditions and rampant popular myths which, over the following years, grew and fed off one another, at least watered the rise of the far-right and of Hitler's *Third Reich* – the Nazis.

There's always a thing behind the thing

On Monday 20th July 2015, a decade on from London's 7/7 terrorist attacks, and with the threat of ISIS building, the British Prime Minister, David Cameron, made a major speech on the deteriorating global situation regarding terrorism, as well as the fight against extremism and radicalisation.

Before I go further, a word of explanation. Through this book I have chosen to use a number of excerpts from Cameron's speech. This is not intended to make my writing any more UK-centric than it already inevitably is – being written from within a UK context. Rather, it is because, in my view, Cameron's content is broadly in line with other Western leaders and at the time of writing is probably the most comprehensive position on terrorism put forward by one of their number. In truth, this issue is one that impacts upon people around the globe, which means that the solutions we find must be 'joined-up' global responses if anything is going to change anywhere.

"When people say, 'It's because of the involvement in the Iraq War that people are attacking the West,'" argued Cameron, *"we*

should remind them: 9/11 – the biggest loss of life of British citizens in a terrorist attack – happened before the Iraq War."

But, there's always a thing behind the thing. The problems of the present are rooted in the decisions of the past. It is the age-old principle of cause and effect.

On 25th July 1990, just days before the Iraqi Army's occupation and annexation of Kuwait (2nd August 1990), which was to lead to the First Gulf War, Saddam Hussein made a speech in which he explained, *"We do not place America among the enemies. We place it where we want our friends to be and we try to be friends. But repeated American statements last year made it apparent that America did not regard us as friends." Five days* earlier, in another speech, he had said, *"The policies of some Arab rulers are American ... They are inspired by America to undermine Arab interests and security."*[15]

Extraordinarily, 25 years on, Saddam's words were to find something of an echo from an unlikely source. Speaking of *'the terrible events of September 11th 2001'*, at the launch of *The Centre on Religion & Geopolitics* and the *'Inside the Jihadi Mind'* report, Tony Blair said, *"One thing is clear certainly to me. This problem had been a long time in the making. The roots date back over half a century and, for sure, they were well watered by the toxic mixture of bad politics and abuse of religion which came out of the Middle East."*

The problem has indeed been a very long time in coming. Past attitudes and decisions by Western governments and Arab states, which stretch back over a century, have had many unintended, yet powerful and emotive consequences.

Few would argue anything other than the UK's involvement in Middle Eastern politics has been destabilising. The secret Sykes–Picot Agreement, for instance, of 1916, which carved up the region to areas of British, French and Russian influence, sowed the seeds of mistrust, denied the Arabs the opportunity to develop proper self-government as the Ottoman Empire came to its end, and has had a lasting and toxic impact.[16]

At the height of this European colonial power, Hilaire Belloc (1870 – 1953) an Anglo-French historian, who became one of the most prolific writers in England during the early 20th century and whose Catholic faith had a strong impact on his works, could make the provocative claim that *'the faith is Europe and Europe is the faith.'* His words betray an attitude that regarded European culture as normative and ultimate, took the link between Christianity, human advancement and western civilisation for granted, and which fostered an air of superiority and arrogance toward all other religions and non-European cultures.

In the post-Second World War period, decisions taken and alliances formed between the West and Saudi Arabia around oil supplies; petro-dollars and Western banks; the West's involvement in middle-eastern building programmes and land distribution; the American response to the 1979 Soviet invasion of Afghanistan; the Western money, weapons and training invested through the 1980s in rebel groups (Mujahideen fighters, including Osama bin Laden) to oppose the Russians; British arms deals with the Saudis; Saudi fundamentalism and the intentional export of militant Salafism to other middle-eastern countries through the establishment of extremist Madrassas (the otherwise popular, everyday word for 'a place of learning and study' in Arabic and various other languages)[17]; bin Laden's developing view that America – *the far enemy* – had corrupted Saudi Arabia with its money and was taking over the heart of the Muslim world ... all these have acted to fuel distrust, anger and radical extremism throughout the Middle East.

As Blair commented at the launch of *Inside the Jihadi Mind*, the research is clear; *"A majority in four large Muslim countries agreed there was a need 'to stand up to America and affirm the dignity of the Islamic people.'"* He also pointed out that the vast majority of those surveyed strongly condemned any violence as an expression of this.[18]

But, this mood of resentment toward America, its allies and their behaviour around the world, has become so commonplace in Muslim countries that it inevitably breeds anger, hostility, hatred, and, in some cases, the strong desire for retribution.

There really is always a thing behind the thing.

Where do we go from here?

We have a problem – a serious one; arguably the biggest threat to peace and stability that the global community faces currently, and it just won't go away.

In his July 2015 speech, Cameron pledged, with echoes of George Bush's *'war on terror'* declaration fourteen years earlier, to defeat the *'poison'* of Islamist extremism with *'tough'* new measures that will *'undermine and eliminate extremism in all its forms.'*

French President, François Hollande thundered similar words in response to the horrifying terror attacks of Friday 13th November 2015 that killed 130 people and left many more seriously wounded in Paris. Making a rare speech to a joint session of the French parliament, he declared, *"France is at war,"* and promised to eradicate terrorism. *"Terrorism will not destroy France, because France will destroy it,"* he said, before going on to propose sweeping new laws and more spending on public safety.

But, even as these words, and many others like them, are spoken, they raise huge underlying questions.

As ISIS watch the likes of Cameron and Hollande make their declarations live on TV, do they or any other terrorist group tremble, panic or gloat? Are they filled with a sense of anxiety or of opportunity? Do they fear our western political leaders or are they using them to drive a giant recruitment campaign?

Do these statements destroy their resolve or simply fuel their fire as it turns terrorists into martyrs and heroes?

And, beyond that, what exactly would an *'effective counter-extremism'* strategy look like? What should we be getting *'tough'* about? And, even more importantly, what should we be promoting in order to build that elusive sense of cohesion?

TWO
Twisted Love

Tuesday 17th February 2015. Three British teenage school-girls from East London, Shamima Begum, Kadiza Sultana and Amira Abase, left their homes before 8am, each giving their family a plausible reason for why they would be out for the day. Instead, they met and travelled to Gatwick Airport to board a Turkish Airlines flight for Istanbul.

Commander Richard Walton, of Scotland Yard's counter-terrorism unit, described the three as '*normal girls*' and '*straight A students*'. In time, however, each contacted their parents to say they were living in Syria, with no plans to return home. Instead, police believed that they were training with ISIS for '*special missions*'.

It's the tip of a large iceberg. In October 2014, Metropolitan police commissioner, Sir Bernard Hogan-Howe, revealed that an average of five Britons travel to Iraq and Syria to join ISIS every week. But how many more are there – choosing not to leave, but to stay and to plot? Hogan-Howe concluded that the '*drumbeat of terrorism in the UK*' was ever-growing '*faster and more intense.*'[19]

Following an Islamic terrorist attack at a Christmas party in San Bernardino, California, in December 2015, which left 14 people dead and injured many more, President Obama warned that the threat from terrorism had *"evolved into a new phase."*

It was Syed Rizwan Farook, aged 28 and born in Illinois, and his wife Tashfeen Malik, 27 who lived locally, and had a 6-month-old daughter whom they left with the baby's grandmother, who carried out the deadly Christmas attack.

The war is everywhere. It has no borders. The enemy is within and is often home-grown. The potential terrorist may not be a formal member of ISIS or al-Qaeda. They could be an individual or a small, dedicated group. You can't see them. You can't bomb them. But the bombs you drop elsewhere in the world will antagonise and anger them.

The situation is the same in Europe. At the beginning of 2015, Hans-Georg Maaßen reported a dramatic rise in the number of active jihadists in Germany. He went on to explain that most of the recruits were men, aged 18 to 30, from migrant backgrounds, who had struggled to adjust to their new lives. Salafism, he said, provided them with a sense of belonging and purpose, *"giving the impression that they will go from being underdogs to top dogs"*.[20]

What kind of *counter-narrative* do we need on which to build a *counter-extremist strategy* that is powerful enough to deal with this new kind of war, and bring real peace to our streets as well as to our wider world?

"It begins. It must begin," declared David Cameron, *"by understanding the threat we face and why we face it. What we are fighting, in Islamist extremism, is an ideology. It is an extreme doctrine. And like any extreme doctrine, it is subversive. At its furthest end it seeks to destroy nation-states to invent its own barbaric realm. And it often backs violence to achieve this aim – mostly violence against fellow Muslims – who don't subscribe to its sick worldview.*

"Some argue it's because of historic injustices and recent wars, or because of poverty and hardship. This argument ... must be challenged....

"Now others might say it's because terrorists are driven to their actions by poverty. But that ignores the fact that many of these terrorists have had the full advantages of prosperous families or a Western university education.

"No – we must be clear. The root cause of the threat we face is the extremist ideology itself."

But, it is perhaps sobering to listen to Eugenio Lilli, of the Department of War Studies at King's College London, on the current situation in the Middle East:

"Unless [the] demands for freedom and economic opportunities are earnestly addressed, the Middle East will remain a region exposed to the risk of cyclical waves of unrest ... Peaceful popular protests have been replaced by bloody conflicts ... The

terrorists' narrative, holding that change in the Middle East can be achieved only through violence, has gained new currency. Tellingly, old (al-Qaeda) and new (Islamic State of Iraq and the Levant) extremist organisations have intensified their activity across the region."[21]

What was it that gave al-Qaeda its impetus before the war in Iraq? What is it that fuels ISIS? Is it simply a case of 'extremist ideology' – nothing more, or less, than an evil, barbaric and twisted version of Islam – or is there more to it?

These are uncomfortable questions that are hard for us to confront. But, if we are to discover a way forward to a lasting peace – either regionally or globally – we cannot afford to ignore them. It's no good trying to tear the head off the poisonous plant of terrorism whilst ignoring its roots. However deep they are, we have to dig down into them in order to 'root out' the causes of the problem we are dealing with. If we will not do this, if we will not do the hard work and learn from the past, we are doomed to condemn ourselves to being trapped in an unending cycle of attack, retaliation, retribution and reprisal.

Too often, in the past, the response of the West to Islam and Islamic fundamentalism has been fuelled, not so much by serious examination and consideration of the range of core issues, but rather by scaremongering in the press and expediency on the part of politicians. Opinions are all too quickly formed with little or no attempt to understand either Islam or traditional Islamic cultural values from an Islamic point of view.

Important questions concerning freedom to insult – such as those posed by tragic events like the killings, at the offices of Charlie Hebdo magazine in Paris, following their publishing of satirical cartoons of Muhammad – end up being answered, on the one hand, by Western secularists with no understanding of Islam, piety or religious devotion, and on the other, by Muslims with little comprehension of how to respond within the framework of a post-modern and pluralist society.[22]

Caricatures and stereotypes abound. Misinformation, over-simplification and sometimes even deliberate lies end up filling the space where honest questions should be posed; ideas should be debated and answers searched for together. For in the absence of this we all end up being blinded by our ingrained ideologies. We need to work hard to rebuild the bridges that are being blown up, not only by terrorists, but also by some of the reporting that surrounds these terrible and terrifying events.

Part of the problem is that most Westerners don't have any meaningful contact with Muslims. Our cultural barriers keep us apart. We therefore end up deriving our understanding of Islam from the media and, as a result, almost inevitably end up with some very twisted and biased views.

Scapegoating

The practice of scapegoating is the oldest trick in the book. ("She did it, not me!" ... "They are to blame, not us!" ... "The problem is all theirs, not ours!").[23] Indeed, it is exactly this that sits at the very heart of the most ancient of stories – the tale of Adam and Eve.

The great anthropologist René Girard developed the concept of what he called '*mimetic theory*' or 'scapegoating' as a way of interpreting the development of human society, culture and behaviour. Since our very beginnings, humans have been driven by mimetic desire (the desire for what others have). Tensions build to a point where society is put at risk. At this point, the scapegoating mechanism is triggered and an individual, or group, is singled out as the cause of the problem – the scapegoat – and forced to carry the blame for it. Social order is restored when people are content that they have dealt with the cause of their problems by blaming and removing the scapegoated individual or group. "*But,*" states Girard, "*although scapegoating provides temporary psychological relief, the cycle always begins again, unless and until it is broken by some deeper and more powerful principle.*"[24]

Although very popular, the '*we're right and they're wrong*' approach to life has never worked. As comforting as it at first seems, it's a mistake to frame huge, multifaceted, issues in over-simplified, binary terms. It is a conversation that ultimately goes nowhere. As Girard said, it just doesn't work because it doesn't deal with the real issues. Life is complex and polarisation is no replacement for the development of real policy and strategy. *"The road to hell',"* commented educationalist Michael Barber, *"is paved with false dichotomies."*

But, when we ruthlessly edit complex stories into simple tales of right and wrong, slowly they become increasingly unconvincing and hollow. They don't make sense anymore and we lose faith in them.

Perhaps the best antidote to the scapegoating on all sides is a deeper, more informed and less reactionary dialogue.

An inconvenient truth

'Bad religion', of course, has its part to play. Without doubt, extreme ideology waters the soil of discontent – we will turn to that later. But, all the evidence suggests that the roots of terrorism are embedded elsewhere.

It was no less a person than John Brennan, the director of the CIA, who, in June 2015, suggested what for many was unthinkable: that the West's foreign policy is one of the key factors motivating those who carry out terrorist attacks.[25]

A few weeks later, a group of 280 academics in the UK, many of whom specialise in radicalisation and conflict, signed a public letter criticising the government's policy *'obsession'* with the *'unsubstantiated view that religious ideology is the primary driving factor for terrorism.'* They argued instead that *'academic research suggests that social, economic and political factors, as well as social exclusion, play a more central role in driving political violence than ideology.'*[26]

Then, in October 2015, when asked if the Iraq war was the *'principle cause'* of the rise of ISIS, even Tony Blair conceded: *"I think there are elements of truth in that."*[27]

Ten years earlier, on Thursday 7th July 2005, three bombs were detonated aboard London Underground trains within 50 seconds of each other at 8.49am. Then, one hour later, a fourth bomb was exploded on the top deck of a number 30 double-decker in Tavistock Square. In all, 56 people were killed, including the four attackers. Over 700 were injured, some very seriously.

The leader, and oldest of the four home-grown suicide bombers, was Mohammad Sidique Khan, from Dewsbury in West Yorkshire. Khan was born in the UK to Pakistani parents who had become British. He grew up in Beeston, a deprived and ethnically mixed area of Leeds. After doing a business studies degree at Leeds Metropolitan University, he worked as a teaching assistant and learning mentor in a primary school with children who were struggling with work or had behavioural problems. Those who knew him described him as gentle and caring.

A few weeks after the 7/7 attacks a 'martyrdom video' emerged featuring Khan – screened by Al Jazeera news – in which he explained:

"I and thousands like me have forsaken everything for what we believe ... Your democratically-elected governments continuously perpetrate atrocities against my people all over the world. And your support makes you directly responsible, just as I am directly responsible for protecting and avenging my Muslim brothers and sisters. Until we feel security, you will be our targets. Until you stop the bombing, gassing, the oppression and torture of my people, we will not stop this fight. We are at war and I am a soldier."[28]

A couple of other home videos, one apparently filmed on November 15th 2004, and a second probably made within days of the attacks, also surfaced and were shown at the inquests into the bombings. Both showed Khan cradling his baby daughter in his arms. In the first he tells his daughter:

"Remember me ... look after mother ... take care of your mother."

In the second he explains:

"Sweetheart, not got too long to go now, and I'm going to really, really miss you ... I actually love you to bits, and you have been the happiest thing in my life, you and your mum .. .I just wish I could have been part of your life, especially growing up these next few months, what with you learning to walk and things ... but I have to do this thing for our future ... and it is for the best I'm sure, in the long run."

Or listen to the voice of Umar Farouk Abdulmutallab, a 23-year-old Nigerian man, explaining his motivation, at his sentencing, for attempting to blow up a Northwest Airlines flight by detonating plastic explosives hidden in his under-wear, on Christmas Day, 2009. The plane was en route from Amsterdam to Detroit and carrying 289 passengers and crew:

"I [attempted] to attack the United States in retaliation for US support of Israel and in retaliation of the killing of innocent and civilian Muslim populations in Palestine, especially in the blockade of Gaza, and in retaliation for the killing of innocent and civilian Muslim populations in Yemen, Iraq, Somalia, Afghanistan and beyond, most of them women, children, and noncombatants."[29]

A twist in the tale

Prof Andrew Silke, a counter-terrorism specialist and advisor to both the UN and the UK Cabinet Office, claims that the UK government's strategy, and indeed that of the West in general, for tackling terrorism is far too focused on ideology, even though there is no evidence to justify their approach. He believes that, instead, the research consistently demonstrates that people are drawn to terrorism more because of *'identity issues'* than extremist ideology.

"The evidence isn't there to say ideology is the prime reason why people are becoming terrorists, and yet ideology is the founda-tion on which the counter-terrorism effort is built … That is a mistake. It is not going to be effective in terms of preventing people becoming radicalised. And it diverts attention from other causes which play a role in why people become involved in terrorism."

In a chapter of *Evolutionary Psychology and Terrorism: New perspectives on political violence*, Silke, and co-author, Dr Rick O'Gorman, set out the evidence for what they call, *'terrorism as altruism'*.[30]

Their work cites interviews with convicted terrorists as well as suicide video messages. They point out that terrorists very often say that they are motivated by wanting to help the people with whom they identify. Silke and O'Gorman explain how those driven by altruistic motives – unselfish concern, or devotion to the welfare of others – can become embroiled in political violence. *"This theme of fighting on behalf of others and in reaction to the suffering of others… recurs frequently in accounts of the personal motivation of individual terrorists."*

"Why would anyone want to take their family to Syria to join Islamic State? Nobody is going to say they are doing it to join the most evil movement that has ever existed," said Silke, who is head of Criminology and director of Terrorism Studies at the University of East London.[31]

"The key message is that you have got to see the terrorists as they see themselves if you genuinely want to understand why people are getting involved. If you talk to terrorists, they portray themselves as altruists – they see it as fighting on behalf of others, whether it's the IRA … or if it's Islamic State."

"We contend that recognising the altruistic dimension to terrorism is essential to fully understanding terrorism, and ultimately, moderating it."

Michael Adebolajo and Michael Adebowale were responsible for the savage and brutal murder of Fusilier Lee Rigby of the Royal Regiment of Fusiliers, on the afternoon of 22nd May 2013, near the Royal Artillery Barracks in Woolwich, South East London. Rigby was off duty and out walking when he was attacked. Adebolajo and Adebowale ran Rigby down with a car, then used knives and a cleaver to stab and hack him to death, before dragging his body into the road. They then remained at the scene until police arrived. It was during this time that Adebolajo, filmed by a bystander, explained:

"The only reason we have killed this man today is because Muslims are dying daily by British soldiers … By Allah, we swear by the almighty Allah we will never stop fighting you until you leave us alone … Through many passages in the Qur'an we must fight them as they fight us …

"I apologise that women had to witness this today, but in our lands women have to see the same. You people will never be safe. Remove your governments; they don't care about you … Do you think politicians are going to die? No, it's going to be the average guy, like you and your children. So get rid of them. Tell them to bring our troops back … leave our lands and you will live in peace."[32]

Silke and O'Gorman's conclusions are shocking. They insist that the weight of the science suggests that most people become involved in terrorism as a result of relatively ordinary social attachments in order to promote, as they see it, the greater good. However unpalatable it is to the rest of the world, their motivation is actually one of misplaced self-sacrifice; the surrender of their own interest in a fight for justice for others.

Accepting this kind of analysis not only goes against accepted wisdom, but it is also extremely uncomfortable. Even more than that, it suggests, in certain circumstances, that ordinary people are capable of becoming terrorists for what they see as virtuous reasons. *"It is counter-intuitive"*, says Silke, *"but terrorism is a really muddy concept. One man's terrorist is another man's freedom fighter."*

Silke's conclusions should come as no surprise to students of theology. As long ago as the 4th century, Gregory of Nyssa, one of the early Church Fathers, explained that evil is perverted love. This *'diseased'* love, he taught, is the *'primary and fundamental cause of propension to the bad, and the mother, so to speak, of all wickedness that follows.'*[33]

At one level, the philosophical and theological question of evil is enormously complex. At another, it is deceptively simple – evil is love gone bad; evil is love perverted; love twisted, love corrupted, love misdirected. It is the impulse, within us all, to relate to one another out of mastery rather than generosity or

31

mutuality which, when left unchecked and allowed to gather steam, will surely destroy us all.

THREE
The Language
of the Unheard

"I contend that the cry of 'black power' is, at bottom, a reaction to the reluctance of white power to make the kind of changes necessary to make justice a reality for the Negro ... I think that we've got to see that a riot is the language of the unheard. And, what is it that America has failed to hear? It has failed to hear that the economic plight of the Negro poor has worsened over the last few years."[34]

The telling words of Martin Luther King, about life in the USA, in 1966, when questioned by Mike Wallace of CBS about an *'increasingly vocal minority'* who disagreed with his commitment to non-violence as a tactic in the fight for civil rights for black Americans. Although King readily admitted that such a minority existed, he insisted that surveys had shown that most black Americans were non-violent. The following year, speaking at Stanford University, he expanded on this same idea:

"... I think America must see that riots do not develop out of thin air. Certain conditions continue to exist in our society that must be condemned as vigorously as we condemn riots. But in the final analysis, a riot is the language of the unheard. And what is it that America has failed to hear? It has failed to hear that the plight of

the Negro poor has worsened over the last few years. It has failed to hear that the promises of freedom and justice have not been met. And it has failed to hear that large segments of white society are more concerned about tranquillity and the status quo than about justice, equality, and humanity. And so, in a real sense, our nation's summers of riots are caused by our nation's winters of delay. And as long as America postpones justice, we stand in the position of having these recurrences of violence and riots over and over again. Social justice and progress are the absolute guarantors of riot prevention. "[35]

If King is right, it raises the question about what, if anything, our Western economies and cultures have learned since then?

All for one and one for all

The term '*globalisation*' is fairly new. It was first penned, it is claimed, by Theodore Levitt, a marketing professor at Harvard Business School, in 1983. Whatever its origins, it is agreed that, defined broadly, it is the process of integrating nations and peoples into a larger community that has increasingly come to describe the overarching political, economic, cultural and religious environment in which we all live.[36]

Everything is changing. Life in the early 21st century sees people around the globe more connected to each other than ever before. Information, money and goods flow more quickly and global communication is taken for granted. An event in one part of the world has immediate implications for the whole world.

Globalisation puts its faith in the idea that free trade, private enterprise and competitive markets promote efficiency and economic growth. It is driven by fast-moving and constantly evolving developments in technology – especially in relation to communications and transportation. It dissolves many of the once formidable barriers of time and distance. It creates vastly expanded flows of money, goods, services, information and people – especially business professionals and skilled workers. It promotes convergence, harmonisation, homogenisation and interdependence.

Globalisation, however, is not only complex, but also controversial. The child that we have given birth to can sometimes behave like a beast! Its demands have huge humanitarian consequences. It begets corporations and multi-nationals that view the world as a single market in which they are free, indeed duty bound, to allocate and reallocate their resources, to shift production and to market goods for efficiency and for their own sustainability and continuous growth. It creates losers as well as winners. It concentrates economic power and the unequal distribution of economic gains as the global super-wealthy pull away from the rest of us. It impacts families, communities, and whole nations.

Globalisation produces social dislocation. It erodes customs, political processes, and ideas. It endangers health. It harms the environment. It turns lush meadows into barren deserts. It pushes those who are winning to dabble in the politics of others in order to protect their oil supplies and other business interests.[37] It leads to the disintegration of indigenous cultures and the loss of sovereignty. It means that many of the pressing issues that we continue to attempt to tackle as though they were isolated, are in fact, interwoven.

Globalisation has no answer to the fact that broken economies, drought and poor harvests, as well as war zones, produce mass migration, which is often not just the logical, but perhaps the only choice. According to the International Organization for Migration (IOM), the number of migrants and refugees crossing into Europe by land and sea in 2015 passed one million. Half were migrants from Syria. A further 3,695 were known to have drowned or were missing at sea.[38]

We have to wake up to the fact that the huge privileges of globalisation bring with them new global responsibilities. They call for a very different way of thinking and behaving from the old internationalist, or nation-state, worldview that enters every discussion confined to a national mindset, based on its own interests. Globalisation is a paradigm shift. In a globalised world, we must learn to think differently; to think about justice and equality for humanity rather than for our local constituency. Tribalism and protectionism have no place at the table. We need a generation of leaders across the world who are capable of taking off their national or corporate 'hats' and thinking about the needs of the whole earth and all its people from an integrated global perspective. A generation of leaders who will, at the same time, respect and protect diversity and difference rather than attempting to impose a 'one size fits all' approach on humanity.

In truth, growing numbers of privileged young Westerners – those who have 'benefited' from the goods of globalisation – are also disillusioned and disenfranchised by it. I was invited recently to talk with senior executives of a leading multinational financial institution. We discussed the ever-growing problem they have with staff retention. They explained that the average age of their staff was just 28, and that their challenge was to address the issue of why 'so much talent' was leaving their employment by its mid-30s. This issue is one which, from my conversations with other large financial organisations, I know is commonplace. As we talked, there was a young Harvard-trained graduate in the room – a staff member – observing the conversation. I asked whether she could relate to the trend we were discussing. Her response was that not only did it sum up her view of things, but it was also the common view of all her young colleagues. *"We will work here to gain experience – but leave to give our lives to something more satisfying and fulfilling, although less well paid."*

It is time for a revolution in geopolitics. Instead of seeing themselves as British or American, Arab or African, Chinese or Russian, Christian or Muslim, or as the representatives of a particular corporate, we yearn for a new breed of world leaders who think of themselves as, first and foremost, human. It's time for nations to do what they find so difficult to do; to approach issues of social justice, equality, peace and sustainability from a more enlightened global perspective with a determination to work together to create a level playing field for all. We speak of inclusive capitalism, now the challenge is to create it.

Some will argue that they are uncomfortable with the idea that poverty, injustice and deprivation are causes of extremism. They will remind us quite rightly that there are billions of people throughout the world who are living in poverty who have not resorted to the kind of heinous violence exhibited by ISIS and other Islamic extremists. In my view, although not the whole story, these are significant contributory factors in creating the soil in which extremism will flourish. When you stretch the elastic band between wealth and poverty too far, resentment, dissatisfaction and anger are inevitable. And, as Martin Luther King commented, in some cases, retaliation and violence are also predictable.

A now famous episode from the British social history of the 1980s highlights this point. In 1985, Margaret Thatcher, the British Prime Minister, was handed a briefing paper in the aftermath of recent rioting in cities including, a month earlier, the Broadwater Farm riot in North London, which resulted in the murder of PC Keith Blakelock.

The five-page memo was co-authored by Oliver Letwin, then a young political adviser, and the former MP Hartley Booth, whilst both were members of the Downing Street policy unit.

It rejected ideas about setting up a £10m communities programme to tackle inner-city problems which, it claimed, would achieve nothing, but only result in vandalism and further unemployment. Instead, it suggested that the unrest was purely due to moral decay, and recommended ways to instil *'better character'* in the population.

This intervention followed a warning from the Home Secretary, Douglas Hurd, following the riots of a *'thoroughly dangerous situation'* in the inner cities. He said that alienated youth, predominantly black, in the inner cities represented *'a grave threat to the social fabric'* of the country.

Hurd told Thatcher in a confidential memo that the Government might have to reconcile itself to the fact that, *"A number of our cities now contain a pool of several hundred young people who we have not educated, whom it may not be possible to employ, and who are antagonistic to all authority. We need to think hard to prevent the pool being constantly replenished."*

But Letwin and Booth urged Thatcher to dismiss suggestions from Hurd and two other cabinet ministers, Kenneth Baker, the Environment Secretary, and David Young, the Education Secretary, to tackle the problem.

Baker, wanted to refurbish rundown council estates and Young, wanted US-*style 'positive action'* programmes to overcome the barriers to jobs and business start-ups for young black people.

Letwin and Booth explained that in their view: *"The root of social malaise is not poor housing, or youth 'alienation' or the lack of a middle class. Lower-class unemployed white people had lived for years in appalling slums without a breakdown of public order on anything like the present scale; in the midst of depression, people in Brixton went out, leaving their grocery money in a bag at the front door, and expecting to see groceries when they got back.*

"Riots, criminality and social disintegration are caused solely by individual characters and attitudes. So long as bad moral attitudes remain, all efforts to improve the inner cities will founder. David Young's new entrepreneurs will set up in the disco and drug trade."

The aides then set out what they said was a programme for creating *'better attitudes'*, including measures to encourage the establishment of *'old-fashioned independent schools'*, and exhorting Mrs Thatcher to bar her ministers from proposing state-funded solutions.

However, at the end of 2015, when the file was released by the National Archives, Oliver Letwin was very quick to issue a statement explaining: *"I want to make clear that some parts of a private memo I wrote nearly 30 years ago were both badly worded and wrong. I apologise unreservedly for any offence these comments have caused and wish to make clear that none was intended."*

50 years on, I believe that Martin Luther King's words remain true. The riot remains the language of some who are unheard. But, what is it that the West has failed to hear? I am convinced that one of the voices we have failed to hear – one of the factors in the growing issue of alienation and extremism – is that the economic plight of the world's poor continues to worsen at the hands of the world's rich.

Inclusive capitalism isn't working. It is time to listen to the cry of the poor, because only as we listen will we find the solutions to the problems we are facing.

FOUR
Bad Religion

'We have just enough religion to make us hate, but not enough to make us love one another', wrote Jonathan Swift in 1711.[39]

In June 2015, Justin Welby, the Archbishop of Canterbury, hosted one of Egypt's most senior scholars and clerics, Professor Ahmad al-Tayeb, the Grand Imam of Cairo's prestigious al-Azhar University. Al-Azhar is regarded as the most important centre of Sunni Muslim theology and al-Tayeb as possibly the most influential Muslim leader in the world.[40]

At a media briefing, at Lambeth Palace, to discuss their joint agenda, Welby spoke of being *"deeply committed to countering the narrative of extremism and terrorism", "a determination to build bridges of peace"* and the need for *"prioritising dialogue ... whether in the region or worldwide."* Al-Tayeb explained that, *"Islam teaches us mercy and Christianity teaches us love and peace,"* and added, *"If we don't have peace among us as religious leaders, then there won't be any peace."* [41]

The courage to be honest
For many years, after any and every new terrorist attack, politicians, security chiefs and law enforcement officers have bent over backwards to explain that Islamist violence has nothing to do with authentic Islam. But, this is the stance that the

British Prime Minister chose bravely to challenge in his July 2015 speech:

"... simply denying any connection between the religion of Islam and the extremists doesn't work, because these extremists are self-identifying as Muslims .... To deny it has anything to do with Islam means you disempower the critical reforming voices; the voices that are challenging the fusing of religion and politics; the voices that want to challenge the scriptural basis which extremists claim to be acting on; the voices that are crucial in providing an alternative worldview that could stop a teenager's slide along the spectrum of extremism."

Cameron's words echoed the stance adopted by Ahmad al-Tayeb, in December of the previous year. In the opening speech of a conference organised by the Muslim World League at the Grand Mosque in Mecca – called specifically to discuss the issue of radicalisation – he told senior clerics from across the Islamic world that it was time to acknowledge that the ideology of the extremists is a *"perversion of the Islamic religion."*[42]

Jihadist factions commit *"barbaric crimes with the clothing of this sacred religion, assuming names such as 'Islamic State' with the intention of exporting their false Islam",* he declared, as he underlined that any terroristic ideology which justifies itself with references to Islam is built around distorted and manipulated understandings of the Qur'an.[43]

Al-Tayeb went on to call for radical reform of Islamic teaching as he made the announcement that al-Azhar University planned to develop and promote studies aimed at tackling the manipulation of Qur'anic writings by launching courses on Islamic formation to resource imams working in mosques around the world. However, he also made it clear that one of the factors that has rendered Islamic State's brand of ideology so toxic, is its habit of pronouncing other Muslims to be apostate. Militant Salafi theology rejects much mainline Islamic scholarship as *'innovation'*, referring to established scholars as *'donkeys of knowledge'*. *"The only hope for the Muslim nation to recover unity,"* he concluded, *"is to tackle in our schools and universities this tendency to accuse Muslims of being unbelievers".*

The truth of al-Tayeb's claims is impossible to deny. As I write, countless thousands of Syrian migrants are now in Europe having fled from the misery perpetrated by all sides on their own people. Why is extremist behaviour practised by one Muslim against another? Why does it appear to be endemic within Islam itself?

This situation highlights another key issue. Islam, of course, is not monolithic. There is no 'one Islam'. It doesn't speak with one voice. It never has done, any more than other religions including the Christian Church. Indeed, the fact that Islam is deeply divided – Sunni and Shia, Saudi and Iranian, Salafi and Alawite, purist and progressive – sits at the very heart of the politics of the Middle East.[44]

In his speech to launch the *Inside the Jihadi Mind* report, Tony Blair said that the ideology of Islamic terrorism *"is based on an abuse of true religious faith; but nonetheless one which is strongly held, highly motivating and whose ideological roots go far wider than we presently want to admit."* The evidence suggests that he is right. He added, *"although the numbers of violent extremists are relatively small, the ideology that they share has a penetration and support which goes far wider; and it is the ideology and not just the violence which we must attack and uproot."*[45]

Religious extremism – whether Islamic or based in any other ideology – finds no more fertile soil than that amongst people who harbour a sense of injustice, and believe they are unheard. It is a complex issue in which socio-economic injustice, lack of education and Western foreign policies all play their part. It slowly takes root in the seemingly unanswered search for voice, identity and hope, which inevitably leads to frustration, resentment and anger. But, the acidic rain that brings such rigorous growth to this deadly poisonous plant is a fundamentalist misreading and distortion of its sacred text.

To attempt to deny this religious dimension to extremism is ultimately to misunderstand the problem, and therefore inevitably, to misconceive the solution. Religion is not incidental to the ideology of Islamic terrorism. The reading of scripture is integral to it, which means that no solution that ignores religion can ever succeed.

The issue of the over-literalistic, manipulation and exploitation of the Qur'an, or any other sacred text, propagated by a 'pied-piper preacher' is, to change the metaphor, the ingredient that makes the whole simmering mix of angst and anger boil over. And it is this problem that we have to undermine by demonstrating its shallowness and lack of authenticity – not to ourselves, but to every young person who is otherwise vulnerable to being caught up in its false hope.

The substance of the report, which Blair introduced through his October speech, is an analysis of the content of the propaganda of three Salafi jihadi groups in the Arabian Peninsula: ISIS, Jabhat al-Nusra, and al-Qaeda. It demonstrates that, *'in large part ... [this material] shares similar creedal characteristics; that these amount to a world view heavily defined by religion ... and that there is a constant and repetitive reference to scripture as providing the faith basis for the acts of violence .... In other words, the extremists do not casually or lightly justify their position on the basis of religious faith; the theological justification is central to recruitment, retention and the fanaticism with which their followers act.'* [46]

It concludes that *'the ideology of Salafi-jihadism is a vital motivating force for extremist violence, and therefore must be countered in order to curb the threat.'* The billion-dollar question is, of course, how?

Prof Louise Richardson, the Vice-Chancellor of Oxford University, whose academic expertise is in terror and counter-terrorism, agrees that terror groups are characterised by a *'highly oversimplified view of the world'* and argues that education is the most effective *'antidote'* to violent extremism.[47]

Speaking in the House of Lords, as part of the debate which led up to Britain's 2015 decision to be involved in airstrikes against ISIS in Syria, Justin Welby, the Archbishop of Canterbury, commented:

"If we act only against ISIL, globally, and only in the way proposed so far, we will strengthen their resolve, increase their recruitment and encourage their sympathisers. Without a far more comprehensive approach we confirm their dreadful belief that what they are doing is the will of God ....

"The Prime Minister's strategy ... rightly recognised that military action is only one part of the answer. But there must be a global, theological and ideological component – not just one in this country – to what we are doing, and it must be one that is relentlessly pursued and promoted.

"... Only a holistic, theological and global policy will achieve our aims. There is much work to be done, but only in this way will the fundamentalist thinking that drives the extremism be shown up for what it is, invalidated and disproven in its own terms. An ideology can only be defeated in terms of ideas."[48]

After the tragedy of the Charlie Hebdo killings in Paris, tribute cartoons to the massacred journalists compared pencils with guns, and writers with fighters. Meanwhile, public demonstrators held pens and pencils in the air.

The phrase *the pen is mightier than the sword* first appeared in the writing of novelist and playwright Edward Bulwer-Lytton in 1839, in his historical play Cardinal Richelieu. In the play, Richelieu, who was the chief minister to King Louis XIII of France, discovers a plot to assassinate him, but as a priest he is forbidden to take up arms against his enemies. Faced with this crisis, his page, François, points out: "*But now, at your command are other weapons, my good Lord.*" Richelieu agrees: "*The pen is mightier than the sword ... Take away the sword; States can be saved without it!*"

FIVE
Unmasking the Deception

As the saying goes – 'any text without a context is a pretext!'

All religion is a dialogue with past texts. The world is waiting for Muslims – as well as Christians and Jews – to engage in a more honest conversation about why and how our sacred texts can be, have been, and sometimes are still read as encouraging aggressive attitudes, endorsing judgmental behaviour and even inciting violence. This difficult but vital task awaits the academics and practitioners of all faiths. We can no longer excuse or disguise it. Indeed, because our behaviours are always – except for the inevitable gap between our aspiration and performance – motivated by beliefs, for every faith community, the study of hermeneutics is perhaps the highest priority.[49]

Hermeneutics is the art and science of textual interpretation. It deals with the complex but vital questions of how a text from another time can speak authentically into our contemporary world. In order to do this, its task is to unearth the cultural and political backdrop into which the text was first written, including the social assumptions and perceptions of its author and the audience to whom it was originally directed. But, it must also examine the presuppositions – both conscious and subconscious – within the present reader's cultural location.

A good hermeneutical approach demands that present day readers of both the Qur'an and the Bible grapple with these vital questions, rather than reading ancient texts superficially without consideration of their original context. That means working hard to understand what was going on in the culture surrounding the writer, as well as the worldview out of which they were writing. Ultimately, it is only the development of these disciplines that can guard an audience against over-literalistic, or over-simplistic, readings of their own, or anyone else's, sacred texts.

Our hermeneutical task is, therefore, far too important to be left to clerics and the world of scholarship alone. Equally important must be the work of those who develop, apply and ground it in the grassroots context of local communities, schools, children's and youth work and the week-to-week life of mosques.

As Blair reminds us: *"There are millions of schoolchildren every day in countries round the world – not just in the Middle East – who are taught a view of the world and of their religion which is narrow-minded, prejudicial and therefore in the context of a globalised world, dangerous."*

Both Christian and Muslim communities must recognise the atrocities that have been committed in the name of their religions, stretching from the Christian holy wars, which began toward the end of the Roman Empire, and continuing through history right up to the present-day threat from

Islamic extremism. Both faith communities must leave behind their ideologies of religious supremacy, and move away from the idea that their tradition has a monopoly on truth. In the words of Dave Andrews:

"... it is absolutely vital for the future welfare of the human family that [Christians and Muslims] examine [their] frequent utter disregard for human rights, diabolical persecution of unorthodox traditions and heterodox religions, and total destruction of 'infidels' in genocidal 'Holy Wars' waged in the name of our 'great God.'"[50]

Some of our priorities must be to:

- Examine our religions as they are actually practised, acknowledging that much violence that has been committed in their name throughout history.

- Acknowledge that we can do more than we have done to date, in recognition of the fact that we do have much influence.[51]

- Create and nurture safe places for face-to-face discussion and relationships between members of our faiths within our communities.

- Challenge stereotypes and suspicion through joint events and projects designed to build a culture of respect around our common humanity.

- Develop far better theological and hermeneutical training for imams and for church leaders.[52]

- Encourage, support and maximise the reach of those prepared and capable of offering an alternative inter-pretation of the theology of Islam and who can rebut the propaganda of the extremists on religious and scriptural grounds.

Reclaiming hidden treasure

Findings in *The Centre on Religion & Geopolitics* report reveal a number of key *'ideological'* values that form the scriptural basis of the actions of the three extremist groups it researched. It explains that justifications from the Qur'an, the Hadith,[53] or from the later writings of Islamic scholars, appear in 87 per cent of the propaganda. It highlights that 63 out of the 114 surahs (chapters) of the Qur'an are quoted in this litera-ture, and also demonstrates that their habit is to 'cherry-pick' passages, without context, which they then read to support their case.

- The importance of *tawhid* (monotheism), the oneness of God, and the one *Ummah* (the global Islamic community), appear in over 74 per cent of the propaganda.

- The importance of honour, and standing in solidarity of the whole Muslim community *(or Ummah),* appears in 68 per cent of the materials analysed.

- An emphasis on the nobility of *jihad* runs throughout the propaganda, often presenting it in chivalric terms. Such references appear in 71 per cent of the propaganda.

- The virtue of martyrdom – applied deliberately to death in battle – forms a significant part of the value of honour, appearing explicitly in 32 per cent of the propaganda, and implicitly in 68 per cent.

The complication is that, in all these cases, the over-literalistic or fundamentalist readings of the Qur'an misrepresent widely-held and helpful theological ideas of Muslim communities around the world, rather than simply denying and rejecting them. Many of the concepts expressed in the propaganda of the terrorist groups echo, but twist, legitimate values celebrated across the various schools of Muslim thought. It is therefore essential that we are very careful to distinguish clearly between authentic understandings of the Qur'an on the one hand, and the distorted interpretations of Islamic fundamentalism on the other.

Through lack of thoughtful appreciation of core Islamic concepts, it is too easy for the West to dismiss and attack Islam itself, rather than focus on the warped version that feeds the poison of extremism. Unfortunately, this is a problem that has often been fuelled by the soundbites of the media and, even more sadly, some politicians. But, worse than that, this very dismissal of precious concepts, principles and beliefs antagonises young Muslims and increases their vulnerability to more radical elements within Islam.

The concept of jihad itself is a perfect example of this extremist twisting. Currently, for many, jihad is viewed as nothing more than a byword for terror (violent 'holy war'). Jihad is, however, an ancient and honourable concept and practice, which pervades the mind and soul of the various strands of mainstream Islam. Its literal meaning is 'struggle' or 'effort'. It is also important to understand that, in the Qur'an, jihad is not the word for war (which is *qital*). For the vast majority of Muslims, it speaks primarily of the inner spiritual struggle to serve Allah and in a secondary sense, of the work of those who follow Islam as they make God known. For them, instead of being understood as an act of abuse or violence, it finds a resonance or parallel with the idea and practice, within Christianity and other faiths, of spiritual disciplines, such as prayer, mediation, service, witness and giving.[54]

Another Islamic concept that has been bastardised by the fundamentalists is that of a Caliphate and a Caliph. As we have seen, in the Muslim world religion permeates everything, so a Caliphate is the idea of the civil and religious aspects of life being integrated rather than separated. And following this integrated understanding of life, the term 'Caliph' is used to refer to a person who fulfils the roles of both civil and religious leader – who is seen as a successor to Muhammad.[55]

The irony is that the concepts of a Caliph and Caliphate are, in fact, very similar to the Catholic ideas of papal succession and what is known as a 'sacerdotal-monarchical' state; the governance system that operates within the Vatican City, where the Pope is the sovereign and absolute monarch over affairs both spiritual and civil.[56]

Equally, and linked to all of this, there is also very widespread support for the concept of Sharia across the various schools of mainstream Islam. Sharia is an archaic Arabic word denoting 'the pathway or steps to be followed'. Sharia, or Islamic law, is derived primarily from the Qur'an and the Hadith, which, once again, integrates both religious and civic duties. Historically, adherence to Sharia has served as one of the distinguishing characteristics of the Muslim faith, although there is, of course, much debate about how this should be interpreted or applied today. At its heart, however, in more progressive Islamic thought, it simply represents a yearning for a more holistic, less hedonistic, more communitarian, less capitalistic, more spiritual, less superficial approach to life.[57]

The elephant in the public square

Can Islam be reformed? Can Islam adapt to the claims of the modern world and remain true to the fundamental texts and beliefs of Islam?

Barack Obama put it this way:

"ISIL does not speak for Islam. They are thugs and killers, part of a cult of death. And they account for a tiny fraction of more than a billion Muslims around the world, including millions of patriotic Muslim-Americans who reject their hateful ideology … Moreover, the vast majority of terrorist victims around the world are Muslim.

"If we're to succeed in defeating terrorism, we must enlist Muslim communities as some of our strongest allies, rather than push them away through suspicion and hate."[58]

But he was very careful to add that his call for reason, *"does not mean denying the fact that an extremist ideology has spread within some Muslim communities,"* or that this is a *"real problem that Muslims must confront without excuse."*

The Islamic community has to address a huge range of specific issues.

Take, for example, the issue of apostasy – the conscious abandonment of Islam by a Muslim. The decision to abandon Muslim faith, convert to another, or marry outside it, has terrible consequences – 'honour-' or 'shame-based' violence and killings – within many traditional Islamic families, communities and countries.

Or, in traditional Islamic law, if a husband of a Muslim couple decides to leave Islam and apostatise, he must be divorced from his wife, since a Muslim woman married to a non-Muslim man is regarded as unacceptable. But if the marriage is otherwise happy isn't this not only inappropriate, but also highly irresponsible?

Or, the question of how, if Islam is a peaceful faith, and Muhammad disdained war, this fits with the rapid spread of Islam through conquest in the hundred years after his death?

Or, what are we to make of jihad's more militaristic interpretations historically? Were they always a mistake, or have they just been overtaken by changing circumstances, and become embarrassing or irrelevant?

Such issues, and hundreds of others like them, must be answered.

The key for the Islamic community in all this is hermeneutics; how to interpret sacred texts, the Qur'an and Hadith in particular, in ways which are faithful but relevant to modern contexts. That's why there are few topics that generate as much controversy within Islam as what exactly constitutes '*bida*', *the Arabic* term for 'innovation'.

One well-attested Hadith teaches that Muhammad told one of his companions to *"Beware of matters newly begun, for every matter newly begun is innovation (bida), every innovation (bida) is misguidance, and every misguidance is in hell."*[59]

So, today, as Muslim scholars around the world ask questions of some of the more over-literalistic or violent exegesis (*tafsir*) of the Qur'an and Hadith, the issue for them is does bida literally mean that any and every innovation in religious matters is unlawful, or is there room for movement?

While fundamentalists regard bida as covering all innovation, or attempts to move away from traditional stances, others think differently and teach that the way of the Prophet was to accept new acts initiated in Islam that were good, and which did not conflict with or contravene established principles of Sacred Law.

The other important concept in this debate is the idea of '*fiqh*'. Fiqh, the Islamic word for jurisprudence (the philosophy and science of law), comes from an Arabic term which means 'deep understanding' or 'full comprehension'.

Muslims believe that Sharia represents divine law as revealed in the Quran and the Sunnah. The Sunnah (literally 'custom' or 'tradition') is the verbally transmitted record not only of Muhammad's sayings, but of what he believed, implied, or tacitly approved or disapproved, as well as various reports about his companions. Sunnah is heavily dependent on Hadith – indeed, by some it is viewed as synonymous with it – since the vast majority of tradition about Muhammad comes from that source, as recorded by his companions.[60]

But, fiqh is the human understanding or interpretation of Sharia as developed by Islamic jurists (judges) and implemented through their rulings (*fatwas*). There are, however, a number of different schools of fiqh, each with its distinctive and often conflicting emphases and practices of interpretation.[61]

In a lecture, which he and Egyptian-Swiss scholar, Tariq Ramadan, gave at Oxford's Sheldonian Theatre in 2010, Shaykh Hamza Yusuf commented that many Muslim leaders lack the intellectual tools to navigate modern situations, even though Islam itself has all the necessary resources for reform – or to use his term, 'renovation'. As one journalist covering the lecture put it, the problem is *'weekend Muftis dishing out fatwas ... without the proper training.'*[62]

The road ahead for the worldwide community

The task before the Muslim community is clear, but equally, without the discipline of good theological and cultural scholarship and dialogue, the West, through lack of insight, understanding and respect, will continue to fall into the trap of dismissing important and wholesome ideas which have a resonance with, and an authentic role within, mainstream Islamic thought.

More than this, the West's urgent task is also to find ways of supporting the numerous Muslim scholars who, from various schools of thought, feel a deep sense of pain at the hijacking of their religion and are already working hard – and bravely – to offer deeper and more authentic understandings of Islamic theology; understandings that are capable of rebutting extremist propaganda on scriptural grounds. Only a counter-terrorism strategy that includes a focus on the religious as well as the political and social can ever prove to be successful in the long term.

SIX
Different Eyes

"We believe in respecting different faiths, but also expecting those faiths to support the British way of life," declared David Cameron. *"... this is how I believe we can win the struggle of our generation. Countering the extremist ideology by standing up and promoting our shared British values .... We should contrast [the extremists'] bigotry, aggression and theocracy with our values. We have, in our country, a very clear creed and we need to promote it much more confidently."*

Thereby hangs a very long tale. Despite the Prime Minister's words, the questions just tumble into your head. What are British values? Is there a definitive list? If not, who gets to decide what's on it? How would we ever all agree on it? I'm not even sure I have the same values as my parents? If there is a list, who compiled it and why don't we know about it? What if we don't agree with it all? Is it the same one that they model in parliament and big business? Who counts as British anyway?

In truth, there is an official – though largely unknown – list of 'Fundamental British Values', first compiled by the government in 2011. It requires UK educational establishments to promote democracy, the rule of law, individual liberty, and mutual respect and tolerance of those with different faiths and beliefs.[63]

But, that is just the problem. Although there is nothing to disagree within them, these values form part of a government document rather than being written into the soul of the people. And, added to that, there's an aching gap between the way of life they suggest and the perceived culture and behaviour even of our institutions themselves; a culture where, for instance, *'the rule of law'* or *'mutual respect'* seem to be drowned out by vested interest, cover-up and scandal and where truth too often seems to end up being sacrificed to media coverage and politics.

All this feels especially acute for those who feel least heard. As a Muslim friend of mine – a former surgeon at a leading UK hospital – told me recently, *"We are asked to contribute but do not feel that we have any representation. Instead, almost every day I read misrepresentations of Islam in the press – both tabloid and broadsheet. If I feel frustrated, imagine what it does to some disempowered, unheard, young people."* Another friend wrote to me with these words, *'As a Muslim living in a modern western society, I feel more honest discussions need to be had rather than narrow-minded finger-pointing and scaremongering policies .... There are many people within the Muslim community who are afraid even to have their opinion, and this is not healthy for society ... the proposed policies to deal with extremism are creating an atmosphere of fear, and a fear of thought police.'*

If one of the fundamentals of 'British values' is to be *'mutual respect and tolerance of those with different faiths and beliefs'* it will require not only a new openness of attitude, but also a genuine commitment to understand and accurately represent the values that are precious to them.

Individualism vs. communal responsibility

Perhaps the most challenging aspect of traditional Islamic culture for secularised Westerners to grasp is just how central the honour of the family and community is to both a Muslim's personal and public identity.

Westerners place huge emphasis on individualism and autonomy. The concept of the 'freedom of the individual' and all that goes with it is central to Western thought. Personal initiative is admired and encouraged. Traditional Muslim social values, however, present a stark contrast. In Islamic thought, Western individualism is by definition, at odds with its understanding of social identity. Rather than valuing and promoting individual rights and decision making, it is the concepts of *tawhid*[64] and *Ummah*[65] – the oneness of God (Allah) and the unity, coherence and oneness of the whole Muslim world under that God – that sit at the heart of an Islamic worldview.

Tawhid is Islam's foremost article of faith, its most fundamental concept. It implies that the cosmos is a unified, harmonious whole, centred around the omnipresent God, and insists that nothing is to be worshipped except this God of everything.

Although much misused and distorted by extremists, Islam's whole world view is built around this one central teaching;

its theology, philosophy, its understanding of public policy, even its understanding of natural sciences. They all seek to explain, at some level, the principle of *tawhid*, which also, more generally, speaks of a commitment to the principles of unification, union, fusion, regularisation; consolidation and amalgamation.

For the Muslim, Islam governs the whole of life. There is no division between public and private. The Western secular idea of the separation of religion from politics, and the privatisation of faith, is totally foreign to the purist Muslim.

'Traditionally, a Muslim is not a nationalist, or citizen of a nation-state; he has no political identity, only a religious membership in the Ummah. For a traditional Muslim, Islam is the sole and sufficient identification tag and nationalism and nation-states are 'obstacles', states Özay Mehmet, in '*Islamic Identity and Development*'.[66]

The Western concepts of independence and individualism are therefore alien to the vast majority of Muslim people, across the various branches of Islam, who worry about their corroding impact on Islamic society. And, it is this impulse that has, in large measure, over the last few decades, given rise to the sense of urgency around the need to stand up to America – and to the West in general – and the influence of its values.

Speaking of the impact of the divergence between Western and Muslim social values, Bill Schwartz asserts, *'I would even state that this paradox is one of the driving forces towards Islamic radicalisation in current times.'*[67]

When Westerners are asked to talk about themselves, their answer is most likely to focus on their career, their ambitions, their lifestyle, their hobbies and other interests, or perhaps their family. Muslims, just like other non-Westerners, in complete contrast, will naturally, almost always, focus their responses around their family, its history, or its status in society, and their place within it. This is where their sense of identity is rooted.[68]

'Individual behaviour is driven by a desire for approval among extended family, particularly elders, while any behaviour that brings shame on the self, the family, or disapproval of the elders, is to be avoided.' explains Schwartz.[69]

Westerners who firmly accept the secular principle that freedom of speech entails freedom for one person to say and do things that could be considered to be offensive by another person, simply fail to grasp the depth of emotional reaction to events, publications, or statements which insult Islam. From an Islamic point of view 'justice' is a far more important political and social concept than the Western emphasis on 'liberty'.

'[Traditional] Islamic society perceives what we regard as a cornerstone of the Western value system 'as rebellion against God's law', argues Tahmina Rashid.[70]

So, whether it is the proposal to burn a Qur'an in a public demonstration, the portrayal of Muhammad as a terrorist in a cartoon, or a NATO soldier using a Qur'an for target practice in Afghanistan, each of these are news stories guaranteed to stimulate great anger among Muslims all over the world, including many of those living in the West. The Islamic mind requires a sense of social responsibility that supersedes the rights of the individual, rather than the responsibility to protect the rights of the individual.

More than that, whenever a non-Muslim does or says something which is perceived as an insult to Islam, many traditional Muslims feel honour-bound to join together in a public demonstration of Islamic identity and solidarity.

'It is essential to many Muslims', explains Schwartz, writing in 2014, *'that they are seen by fellow Muslims to be supportive of the honour of Islam. Indicative of this, in the past few years and partly in response to these blasphemous events, different versions of 'bumper stickers' in Arabic have appeared in different countries of the Middle East expressing versions of sentiment like, 'On the honour of my mother and father I will defend you, O my Prophet, to the death'. They have become popular among conservative Muslims ...*

'Criticism, or worse – ridicule, of Islam, the Prophet, the Qur'an, is [therefore] guaranteed to be received in a very negative way and is often interpreted as blasphemy. In many Islamic countries blasphemy laws carry the penalty of death. Blasphemy is a serious charge even in countries where the death penalty is not proscribed.'[71]

Some, therefore, feel honour-bound to react in very strong, even violent ways. To protest is a statement to fellow Muslims about the sanctity of Islam, the Qur'an, and the honour of the Prophet and of the Islamic Ummah.[72]

Individualism vs. individuality

In Western thought, the emphasis on individualism and autonomy is often critiqued for the weaknesses it creates in our understanding and practise of community. In his classic book *'Christianity Rediscovered'*, Vincent Donovan, an American Catholic priest, who spent 20 years working amongst the Masia – a people of yet another distinctive faith – on the plains of Tanzania in East Africa, offered a commentary on one of the outcomes of this situation. He says of the diversity of life and culture across America that the one *'common denominator'* is *'competition within the group'*.

'An individual's worth within any group is pretty much determined by his or her achievements, talents, skill, or beauty. And even if one is talented, it can sometimes be very difficult to be recognised because of the fierceness of competition present. The endowments and talents that are present are often envisaged

not as contributions to a community, but as additions to one's personal stature. Such are the bitter-sweet fruits of intense individualism.'[73]

In traditional Muslim thinking, Western individualism lends itself to the development of this unhealthy competitiveness, which turns every other person into a competitor. It is important, however, to understand alongside this, that purist or traditional Islamic culture does not seek to undermine or negate individuality or talent, which are not only recognised, but also celebrated as marks of pride for the whole community rather than for what is viewed as individual aggrandisement and destructive competition.

Donovan explains that when he experienced African communities for the first time, one of the things he noticed about them was this same lack of competition within a community:

'No one really tried to stand out in a community, perhaps did not even want to. There was no particular value attached to standing out, as an individual, that is. The most beautiful girl was simply recognised as such, and was a mark of pride for the community that produced her. Everyone would point out the greatest athlete, or the best dancer and rested hopes on such gifted people to bring honour to the village or the community ... The very notion of being chief ... of an age group was not a sought-after honour, even though it implied a nobility of character and personality ....

'Talents that people possessed and displayed were accepted and recognised by the community, and put to good use by the community. People with lesser talents were accepted as such and were expected to contribute according to their ability. No one was rejected for lack of talent.'

There is a huge difference between the concepts of 'individuality' and 'individualism', and, in truth, the Bible also knows nothing of the 'individualism' which has become such a dominant feature of our Western world today. Rather than conceiving of people in overly-individualistic terms, it consistently views them as 'interdependent'; inherently connected to each other. Take, for instance, the famous words from the first chapter of the whole Bible:

'Then God said, "Let us make humanity in our image, in our likeness"... So God created humanity in his own image, in the image of God he created them; male and female he created them.'
– Genesis 1:26-27

Although it usually goes unnoticed, these words do not address individuals as individuals in the sense in which we so readily use that term today. Instead they insist that the divine image characterises and defines humanity as a whole. The image of God is related to all men and women – *'Let us make humanity in our image, in our likeness'.*

The Apostle Paul makes this same point to the young Christian community living in the 1st century city of Corinth, *'Now*

71

you are the body of Christ, and each one of you is a part of it.' He goes on to explain that whatever gift a person uses, *'everything must always be for the common good'*. Our individuality is to be celebrated, but it is a gift designed to build community and interdependence rather than fuel individualism and independence that is centred on its own interest.

A Muslim friend of mine, expressed it like this. *'In Islam, the individual is all important because he or she is meant to anchor around the immovable Qur'an. And, when everyone does this, then the community is one.'*

'Likeness to God cannot be lived in isolation', wrote the Christian theologian Jurgen Moltmann, *'It can only be lived in human community.'*[74]

Perhaps we all have some serous thinking to do!

SEVEN
An Unpalatable Truth

Even as I write these words, the first reports are emerging of an attack by a lone gunman on a Planned Parenthood clinic in Colorado Springs, which has left three people – two civilians and a police officer – dead, after a long standoff.[75]

Another nine people were injured – five police officers and four civilians. Some staff escaped harm by following security protocol and hiding in specially designed 'safe areas' within the building. The clinic provides abortion services and family planning.

Although police at the scene are declining to discuss the gunman's motivations, the president of the Rocky Mountains chapter of Planned Parenthood, Vicki Cowart, has just suggested that the climate of rancour surrounding abortion in the United States has set the stage for such violence.

"We share the concerns of many Americans, that extremists are creating a poisonous environment that feeds domestic terrorism in this country," she said.

The Colorado Springs clinic has, my radio tells me, been the target of repeated protests by anti-abortion activists over the last few months.

Vicki Saporta, president and chief executive of the National Abortion Federation, is saying that her organisation had feared such an attack for some time.

"This clinic is part of the Planned Parenthood Rocky Mountains affiliate, which was featured in one of the highly-edited smear videos released this summer. Since that video, the affiliate has seen an increase in protesters, and death threats against one of their doctors.

"Although anti-abortion groups may condemn this type of violence when it happens, the way that they target and demonise providers contributes to a culture where some feel it is justifiable to murder doctors, simply because they provide women with the abortion care they need.

"Since 1977, there have been eight murders, 17 attempted murders, 42 bombings, 186 arsons, and thousands of incidents of criminal activities."[76]

Radicalisation is not an Islamic problem. It is a human problem that knows no boundaries or doctrinal barriers.

Whilst it remains true that, in our contemporary world, Islamist extremism presents a unique and unparalleled threat to global security – both in scale and ambition – that's not the whole story. The unpalatable truth is that conservative and fundamentalist views within Christianity, which also often fuel judgementalism, exclusion and oppression, in extreme cases, still lead to violent atrocities, even today.

Schwartz writes about this sobering parallel in his book. Speaking of Salafism he explains '... *this 'purist' presentation of Islam purports to represent Islam to all Muslims and to the rest of the world, in much the same way that post-denominational and 'evangelical' Christianity often purports to represent true Christianity, often denying the validity of any other Christian expression or tradition.'*

Pressing his point further, he adds: *'More and more commonly, conservative Christians are labelling mainline, liberal theological perspectives as 'unbiblical' or 'apostate', advocating separation as necessary to maintaining the purity of Christian faith. We have seen this polarisation in different waves during controversies over creation, women in ordination, women in the episcopate, ordination of homosexuals, and in general, the literal interpretation of biblical texts.'*[77] And, to his list you could also add, amongst others, same sex marriage, migration (*'Muslim refugees who will undermine Europe's Christian roots'*), xenophobia and abortion.

Bounded and Centred sets

Within the tradition of Christianity, as well as Islam, there are those who operate in what Paul Hiebert, a theologian and anthropologist based at Fuller Theological Seminary in California, first defined in 1978, as 'bounded-set' religion. He contrasted this with what he termed an 'open-set' approach.[78]

Hiebert drew on the world of maths, where sets are categories defined by structural characteristics and boundaries. He then applied this thinking to the world of religion. He listed characteristics of bounded sets; created by listing the essential characteristics an object must have in itself to belong to the set; defined by a clear boundary, and only containing objects that are uniform in their essential characteristics – constituting a homogeneous group.

Bounded sets, he said, are essentially static – they have to do with the ultimate, changeless structure of reality. They are defined in terms of unchanging, universal, abstract categories. The central question they raise is, therefore, whether an object is inside or outside their category.

If we think of 'religion' as a bounded set, we focus on external characteristics, such as assent to doctrinal orthodoxy. We become obsessive about boundary maintenance and inquisitorial judgments about whether persons and groups are in or out. We work to maintain the sharpness of the boundary, because the boundary is critical to maintaining the category.

'Bounded set' religionists are therefore given to dogmatism, judgementalism, and intolerance of dissent. Their closed perspective has dangerous implications because, committed to unchanging and unchangeable ideologies, they not only draw lines of demarcation through the human race, but also feel a responsibility to impose their views on all others.

By contrast Hiebert defined centred sets as a grouping of things on the basis of how they relate to other things, not what they are in and of themselves; they are created by defining a centre or reference point and the relationship to that centre; they do not have sharp boundaries that separate the objects within the set from those outside it. Centred sets are dynamic rather than static; there is room for variation, things headed away from the centre can shift and turn toward or away from the centre.

'Centred-set' religionists do not regard themselves as having a monopoly on God, or an exclusive franchise on the truth, and therefore include 'the other' in ways that are empathic and respectful and don't lead to judgementalism or violence, but instead works for the non-violent resolution of conflict through dialogue.

Only those who pay no attention to the history of Christianity or current affairs can dismiss this point. Both consciously and subconsciously, our beliefs shape our behaviours. Our foundational attitudes always find expression, one way or the other, in our reactions and responses. Our core values have consequences in terms of our actions. Put differently, the narrative or story we believe will always shape who we become. Here are some examples:

Europe: On 22 July 2011, 'lone wolf' Anders Behring Breivik, a baptised and confirmed Norwegian Lutheran, killed eight people by setting off a van bomb parked next to government buildings in Oslo, Norway. He then went on to kill a further 69 young people at a summer youth camp, on the island of Utøya. In his self-published book, '*2083 – A European Declaration of Independence*', he revealed that his actions were fuelled by his belief that Europe's Protestant churches had sold out to a leftist and pro-immigration agenda and that even the Pope had abandoned Christianity. Driven by militant Islamophobia, he calls Islam '*the enemy*', and argues for the violent annihilation of multiculturalism as well as for the deportation of all Muslims from Europe.[79]

America: The Ku Klux Klan is the white Protestant-led, racist, anti-Semitic movement with a commitment to extreme violence to achieve its goals of racial segregation and white supremacy. Its bastardised version of the Christian story, which embraces white hoods, burning crosses and lynchings, means that amongst the various right-wing hate groups that exist in the United States, the Klan is still the most prominent.[80]

The Klan first emerged in 1866, following the end of the Civil War, as America's first true terrorist group with an explicitly religious foundation based in a Christian ideology.[81] '*Jesus*' they taught, '*was the first Klansman*'.[82] Their ritual of burning crosses, accompanied by prayer and hymn singing, is steeped in Christian symbolism and tradition. Aside from intimidating their victims, it was designed to demonstrate their respect and reverence for Jesus.[83] At first, the Klan famously focused its anger and violence on African-Americans, on white Americans who stood up for them, and on the federal government that supported their rights. Their methods included arson, beatings, the destruction of property, lynching, murder, rape, tar-and-feathering and whipping – as well as intimidation via such means as cross burning.

Subsequent incarnations of the Klan – which, once again, studies show typically emerge during times of rapid and disorientating social change – have added more categories to its list of enemies including Jews and Catholics. Currently, however, experiencing another period of growth, the Klan's focus has switched to the Lesbian, Gay, Bisexual and Transgender (LGBT) community, as well as immigrants in general and specifically Hispanics.

Africa: In 2014, Amnesty International reported several massacres in the Central African Republic committed by the Anti-balaka – a group of Christian militias – against Muslim civilians, forcing thousands to flee the country, after the rise to power of Michel Djotodia in 2013.[84] By March 2015, it was reported that these groups had also destroyed almost all the mosques in the Central African Republic.[85]

Africa: Another group currently active in the Central African Republic is the Lord's Resistance Army. Originally a Ugandan guerrilla army, the LRA has been involved in terrorist acts in the north of that country since the mid-1980s. It now also operates in South Sudan and the Democratic Republic of the Congo, with a stated goal of ruling according to the Ten Commandments. It has been accused of numerous crimes against humanity; including abductions, mutilation, torture, rape, and using forced child labourers as soldiers, porters, and sex slaves, and various massacres. Mixing aspects of Christian beliefs with its own brand of spiritualism, it is led by Joseph Kony, who proclaims himself the spokesperson of God and a spirit medium of the Holy Spirit. LRA fighters wear rosary beads and recite passages from the Bible before battle.

During an interview given to the Integrated Regional Information Networks news agency, Vincent Otti, Kony's deputy, was asked about the LRA's vision of an ideal government, to which he responded:

"Lord's Resistance Army is … the name of the movement, because we are fighting in the name of God. God is the one helping us in the bush. That's why we created this name, Lord's Resistance Army. And people always ask us, are we fighting for the Ten Commandments of God? That is true – because the Ten Commandments of God is the constitution that God has given to the people of the world. All people."

The continuum to terror

It is indisputable that the reach and influence of Islamic fundamentalism is far wider than the terrorist group and that, especially for some vulnerable young people, this can create a conveyor belt to extremism. But, in exactly the same way, the poisonous tentacles of Christian fundamentalism continuously do their dehumanising work.

The battle of America's Civil Rights Movement was fought against the backdrop of the infamous decision, in 1959, of Judge Leon M. Bazile, a lifelong conservative Catholic, who declared that the interracial marriage of Richard and Mildred Loving (a white man and a black woman) was illegal. Sentencing them to one year in prison, suspended for 25 years on condition that they leave the state of Virginia, he made his explosive statement:

"Almighty God created the races white, black, yellow, malay and red, and he placed them on separate continents. And but for the interference with his [arrangement] there would be no cause for such marriages. The fact that he separated the races shows that he did not intend for the races to mix."[86]

In an African context, what should we say of the religious conservatism of those Christians who consistently opposed the ANC whilst continuing to promote a theology that legitimised the Apartheid system – the institutionalised segregation of the South African people according to their race?

The Dutch Reformed Church was the most powerful religious institution in South Africa. All of the country's Presidents and Prime Ministers during the apartheid years were members. Indeed, it was only in 1992, two years after the release of Nelson Mandela from prison, that the denomination was willing to acknowledge its teaching of apartheid as a sin.

And still today, the tragedy is that there are many who preach hatred, division and hostility in the name of the Church. One prominent example – with global influence – is Franklin Graham, the son of the great preacher and wonderfully gracious Dr Billy Graham, who now heads his father's Christian evangelistic organisation. As recently as December 2014 he has described Islam as a *'religion of war'*, making it clear that he has not softened his stance since he controversially referred to Islam as a *'very wicked and evil religion'* in the wake of the 9/11 attacks in 2001. *"This is Islam. It has not been hijacked by radicals. This is the faith, this is the religion. It is what it is. It speaks for itself."*

George Bernard Shaw once quipped: *"God created man in his image – unfortunately man has returned the favour."*[87] It is sobering to witness how, in the 21st century, there are many who continue to use 'their religion' – worn like a badge of identity – to divide and oppose.

EIGHT
Time to Talk

Three and a half billion people – half the world's population – profess Christianity or Islam.

The tragedy is that, historically, most literature written by Christians about Islam, or by Muslims about Christianity, has been either polemic or apologetic in nature. Indeed, it has usually been written as a resource for a readership that sees interfaith encounters purely as a smokescreen to preach, proselytise and recruit the other side to their cause. The problem is, of course, that any presentation of one religion through the filter of the values and theology of another is bound to misrepresent the 'other'.

In this context, although it seems obvious, it is worth making the point that Islam is not like Christianity, or vice versa. Traditional and popular comparisons between the two have often fallen into the trap of, for instance, equating the roles of Jesus and Muhammad, or the Qur'an and the Bible, or Lent and Ramadan. Not only are these conclusions very inaccurate, but also they inevitably reinforce misunderstandings on both sides.

The three monotheistic faiths – Judaism, Christianity and Islam – all refer to the one true, universal, creator God[88] and trace their roots back to the same man: Abraham.[89] And,

as both the Qur'an and the book of Genesis record, as part
of this, Abraham was given a promise by the one God of
everyone and everything:

'He [Allah] said, "I am appointing you as the leader of humanity."'
– Qur'an 2:124

'I [God] will make you into a great nation,
  and I will bless you;
I will make your name great,
  and you will be a blessing ….
and all peoples on earth
  will be blessed through you.' – Genesis 12:2-3

This Abraham was not Jew, Christian, or Muslim, but he
is the father of all. Perhaps, therefore, the starting place for
dialogue between the three Abrahamic faiths is to take a fresh
look at this ancient prophecy delivered to Abraham, and
consider our joint track record on living up to it. Are we a
'blessing' to humanity? Do we offer clear moral and spiritual
leadership to the nations of the world? Or, does this prophecy
remain unfulfilled? The ultimate question must therefore be
simply this: will our generation play its part in moving toward
its fulfillment through the courage and trust we are willing to
demonstrate in taking steps towards one another? Or is our
legacy one wherein we are to be tragically remembered only
as having been part of the problem?

Do we all worship Allah?

In the 6th century, Muhammad unified Arabia into a single religious movement: Islam. As a result, Muslims consider him to be the restorer of the uncorrupted original monotheistic faith of Adam, Noah, Abraham, Moses, Jesus and other prophets.[90]

As part of this, some scholars suggest that Muhammad deliberately used the term 'Allah' for the name of God specifically, to establish common ground and understanding in addressing Arabs, Jews and Christians. Indeed, it is a fact that long before Islam existed, the name '*Allah*' was used by Arab Christians to refer to the one true God.[91]

From a Christian perspective, Fouad Accad, who worked for the Bible Society in Lebanon, the Middle East and Gulf, offers an interesting commentary on this:

'Some Christians unthinkingly say, 'Allah is not God'. This is the ultimate blasphemy to Muslims, and furthermore, it is difficult to understand. Allah is the primary Arabic word for God. It means 'The God.' There are some minor exceptions. For example, the Bible in some Muslim lands uses a word for God other than Allah (Farsi and Urdu are examples). But for more than five hundred years before Muhammad, the vast majority of Jews and Christians in Arabia called God by the name 'Allah'. How, then, can we say that Allah is an invalid name for God? If it is, to whom have these Jews and Christians been praying?

And what about the 10 to 12 million Arab Christians today? They have been calling God 'Allah' in their Bibles, hymns, poems, writings, and worship for over nineteen centuries. What an insult to them when we tell them not to use this word 'Allah'! Instead of bridging the distance between Muslims and Christians, we widen the gulf of separation between them and us when we promote such a doctrine.'[92]

It could also be added that the Arabic 'Allah' comes from the original Aramaic, which appears in the Aramaic portions of the Old Testament, and is the very word Jesus would have used in referring to God.

Whenever this view is postulated, however, there are some – both Christians and Muslims – who loudly protest. Those who raise objections generally agree that Christians and Muslims worship *one* God, but will not accept the statement that they worship the *same* God. This issue is far more common amongst Christians than it is Muslims, because once a Muslim is ready to acknowledge that God can be known by a name other than the Arabic 'Allah', they will usually agree that Christians and Muslims worship 'the same God.' Indeed, the Qur'an insists that Muhammad and his followers worship the same God as the Jews:

'Do not dispute with the People of the Book except in a manner which is best, barring such of them as are wrongdoers, and say, 'We believe in that which has been sent down to us and has been

sent down to you; our God and your God is one [and the same], and to Him do we submit.' Qur'an 29:46[93]

At the same time, however, Muslims will also insist that Christians err in 'associating' others with God – i.e. Jesus, the Holy Spirit, and, sometimes based on a common misunderstanding related to a verse in the Qur'an, Mary![94]

The problem as it confronts Christians is, however, of a different nature altogether. Can you say you are worshipping the same God when you have such different understandings of the nature of God? Whilst Christianity and Islam may have the same starting point in the word 'Allah', the point is that it is what is said about this 'Allah' that counts, and their descriptions are poles apart. So, in Franklin Graham's view, for instance, *"The God of Islam is not the same God of the Judaeo-Christian faith."*

It is extremely interesting to observe that, even in rejecting the erroneous concept of God held by the ancient people of Athens, the Apostle Paul had a different approach. Far from rejecting the word the Athenian philosophers, with whom he was debating, used for God, which was 'theos' – the common Greek word for God, he embraced its use. As a result, not only did it become fully absorbed into the language of the 1st century Church but today it is also at the heart of our English word 'theology'!

Writing from a Christian perspective, but in dialogue with leading Muslim scholars and leaders from around the world, the primary argument of Miroslav Volf's book '*Allah: A Christian Response*' is that Christians and Muslims both worship the same God – the only God: the one, true creator God, who is good and calls people to love him and their neighbours.[95]

Whilst not avoiding or minimising the significant differences in Christian and Muslim theology, such as the Trinity, or whether the adjective 'merciful' (dominant in the Qur'an), or the noun 'love' (dominant in the Bible), is the most accurate description of God's primary orientation toward humanity, Volf highlights the significant extent to which both faiths have a common understanding of the nature of God, as well as of how to respond to God in worship. He goes on to urge us to understand that in the light of this, not only respectful dialogue but also mutual cooperation should be the natural outcome.

At the same time as acknowledging that differences between the two religions will always require them to remain separate rather than one, Volf calls on Christians and Muslims to work together for the common good of humanity.[96]

Learning to dialogue

All too often, formal conversations between Muslims and Christians fall into one of three traps. They end up being about the attempt to convert one another; they seek primarily to identify only what is held in common and reduce the discussion to a recognition of our sameness – our belief in one God, our common heritage through Abraham etc.; or they focus solely on areas of common practical concern and opportunity for mutual cooperation, such as a relief effort, the need for religious education in schools, or English language tuition for immigrants.

While this is all healthy, there is a huge difference between social and community cooperation and dialogue. Muslim/Christian dialogue *'must achieve more than simply find ways to co-exist despite our differences.'*[97] We need to recognise that the rest of the world holds us accountable to find the space to discuss our differences, as communities and as individuals, and to work at developing relationships that are honest, frank and open about disagreement, yet committed to one another as human beings.

'Real and honest dialogue requires identification of the distinctive features in our religious traditions that make us different. [Our] conversation lacks integrity if we ignore the fact that there are many values, traditions and doctrines that distinguish us as very separate communities with very different traditions and values.'[98]

A conversation is never a genuine dialogue unless it includes an interest in, and a willingness to understand, the other. Dialogue is only effective to the degree to which the communication is based on mutual understanding. Two, one-way conversations, which happen to take place at the same time in the same room, do not make a dialogue, or even a debate. Dialogue requires openness to criticism, to critical analysis and to an appreciation of what is admirable in each other's faith traditions.

Schwartz makes the telling but difficult point that in genuine dialogue we *'also must admit aspects of our own religious tradition that contribute to (or even promote) radical extremes, bigotry and violence.'* He insists that *'Real dialogue requires honesty, courage and vulnerability, critical introspection, identification of differences and a level of respect that gives room for those differences to co-exist.'*[99]

What's more, healthy dialogue is, by nature, open-ended. It involves attitude and process rather than a tightly-defined programme with specified outcomes. It is a process of discovery and of building relationships. It requires learning to express ourselves, and our beliefs in new ways, using new metaphors that communicate accurately and clearly in order to be understood by others more fully. It also demands new language, which allows us to think and articulate new thoughts.

As Martin Luther King Jr wrote shortly before his death:

'We have inherited a large house, a great 'world house' in which we have to live together – black and white, Easterner and Westerner, Gentile and Jew, Catholic and Protestant, Moslem and Hindu – a family unduly separated in ideas, cultures, and

*interest, who, because we can never again live apart, we must
somehow learn to live with each other in peace.*

'We must learn to live together as brothers or perish together as fools.'

The burka vs. the bikini

Westerners who live in Islamic countries invariably discover
that the piety of Muslims, even those who are casual about
their faith, is inspiring. But they also discover that many
Muslims believe that Christians (a term they assume to be
synonymous with 'Westerners') are predisposed to a lawless-
ness and permissiveness that breeds immorality and the
promotion of a level of individuality that contributes to social
disintegration. They are also very fearful that this influence,
if allowed to, will corrupt their historic values and traditions.
And, although, it is true that the vast majority of Muslims
living in the West enjoy the personal and economic freedoms
of a secular democracy, at the same time many of them are
still very uncomfortable with some of its characteristics.

On the other hand, for Westerners, traditional customs
in Muslim society such as arranged marriages and social
mandates about appropriate dress are perceived as an affront
to the personal autonomy and freedom of the individual.

In other words, Westerners and Muslims continually miscom-
prehend each other's values because each typically encounters
the 'other' through the lens of their own cultural and religious
presuppositions.

There is a poignant cartoon that shows two women – one a Westerner dressed only in a tiny bikini and a fashionable pair of sunglasses, and the other covered from head to foot in a burka – glancing at each other as they pass in the street. A thought bubble coming from the Westerner reads *'Everything covered but her eyes. What a cruel, oppressive, exploitative, male-dominated culture she lives in.'* In the very same moment, a thought bubble coming from the Muslim woman reads *'Nothing covered but her eyes. What a cruel, oppressive, exploitative, male dominated world she lives in.'*

I once heard a young Muslim woman explain to the group she was addressing that the cultural problems facing young Islamic people were not to do with too much Islam, but instead with a lack of it. *"Islam raises the status of the woman. We need to be proud of this, not on the defensive. We need to return to Islam and some values worth living by!"*

From a Christian perspective, Miroslav Volf refuses to shy away from the ethical questions that face contemporary Islam. He suggests that it is impossible to ignore the fact that the punishment for disobedience in the Qur'an is much more severe than in the Bible and that God's love is less obvious in the Qur'an than the Bible. The adjective 'merciful' is far more central to the Qur'an's understanding of God's primary orientation toward humanity than the noun 'love' that is central to the Bible's narrative.

Volf also challenges the relationship of the vast majority of Muslims to violence, who as a whole, still insist on punishing conversion to another religion. He points out that Muslim teaching forbidding apostasy is incompatible with an attitude that acknowledges *'our God and your God is one'* and seeks to respect freedom of religion.[100]

As the Qur'an itself famously explains, we were made into different peoples not that we might despise each other, but that we might understand each other:

'O men! Behold, We have created you all out of a male and a female, and have made you into nations and tribes, so that you might come to know one another. Verily, the noblest of you in the sight of God is the one who is most deeply conscious of Him. Behold, God is all-knowing, all aware.' Qur'an, 49:13[101]

In *'Christianity Rediscovered'* – a book that has become a classic in how to begin real and genuine dialogue across cultural divides – Donovan, reflecting on lessons learned from his work with the Masia, comments:

'… do not try to call them back to where they were, and do not try to call them to where you are, as beautiful as that place might seem to you. You must have the courage to go with them to a place that neither you nor they have ever been before.'[102]

Dialogue eliminates fear. Fear eliminates dialogue. The West has much to learn from the Arab world and vice versa. This moment may be an agonising labour; a painful giving birth, but if we can overcome prejudice and learn the art of dialogue, perhaps the child that is born of our struggle will be beautiful, peace-loving and strong.

NINE

How I was Radicalised

'*Our chief want is someone who will inspire us to be what we know we could be*', wrote Ralph Waldo Emerson, the great American poet.

In 2008, under the last UK Labour Government, the Department for Children, Schools and Families published the '*Learning Together To Be Safe*' toolkit for UK schools. Still available as a resource, it explains carefully that the decision by a young person to become involved in violent extremism, '*may be driven by the desire for adventure' and excitement*'![103]

In the same vein, the UK's current Prime Minister, David Cameron, commented: *"So when groups like ISIL seek to rally our young people to their poisonous cause, it can offer them a sense of belonging that they can lack here at home, leaving them more susceptible to radicalisation and even violence against other British people to whom they feel no real allegiance ... [this] can seem energising, especially to young people. They are watching videos that eulogise ISIL as a pioneering state taking on the world that makes celebrities of violent murderers. So people today don't just have a cause in Islamist extremism; in ISIL, they now have its living and breathing expression."*

The key he said, is *"the question of identity"*, adding that our task *"must be to build a more cohesive society, so more people feel a part of it and are therefore less vulnerable to extremism."*

If that is true, rather than simply attempting to build a defence against the threat of radicalisation through anti-radicalisation strategies – such as that prescribed in the UK by the Government's CONTEST and PREVENT initiatives – we should also be prioritising how we can imbibe a deeper, and more powerful, sense of purpose, identity, meaning and belonging into the lives of vulnerable young people in our communities.[104]

Nature abhors a vacuum. So, rather than making our overall battle one to 'prevent' radicalisation, instead our priority should be to 'encourage' or 'inspire' it. I believe that the primary answer to the problem of radicalisation is, in fact, radicalisation; radicalisation into a positive and compelling narrative that is worth living by. I know that it sounds shocking, but it is only owning a healthy and life-affirming story, which creates the resilience, that will guard against a warped and destructive one. *'Find a purpose: the means will follow'*, the saying goes. Or, to put it in the words of Catholic writer, Richard Rohr, *'When you get your, "Who am I?" question right, all of your, "What should I do?" questions tend to take care of themselves.'*[105]

The problem is that many young Muslims living in the UK, and elsewhere in the West, stare this issue of identity in the face every day. Does being British mean a loss of Muslim identity? How can you live as a good Muslim in a country where Islam is not the majority faith and where you feel a lack of representation, or of being heard? For a healthy sense of identity, everyone needs to feel that they have a place; that they can contribute to the society of which they are a part, and that their contribution is appreciated. And, the fact that so many young Muslims, as well as those of other cultures, do not feel that they have a place or voice in mainstream society is at the very heart of the problem.

'Neither revolution nor reformation can ultimately change a society,' said Ivan Illich, the Austrian philosopher and Roman Catholic priest. *'Rather you must tell a new powerful tale, one so persuasive that it sweeps away the old myths and becomes the preferred story, one so inclusive that it gathers all the bits of our past and our present into a coherent whole, one that even shines some light into the future so that we can take the next step forward. If you want to change a society, then you have to tell an alternative story.'*[106]

In my book *'Being Human'*, I pick up on this theme: *'Each and every one of us lives in search of a convincing story that explains to us who we are; an overarching narrative that supplies us with a sense of worth and direction; a sense of purpose that wakes us up'.*[107] I explain that without a compelling overarching story – a sense of who we are and where we fit – we are lost.

Read these words from the recruitment section of the British Army website.

'It's a job where no two days are the same. Where travel and adventure go with the territory. Where you work with people who become lifelong friends … everyone has the opportunity and support to succeed.'

'The Army is different from most jobs. The people you work alongside aren't just your colleagues, they're your best mates … you get somewhere to call home.'[108]

Why do young people join ISIS? Have we ever considered that it may well be for many of the same reasons they join a regular army?

This, of course, is exactly why the issues of good hermeneutics and clear communication are essential to both Islam and Christianity. We need to take responsibility for articulating better, bigger, more life affirming, inclusive and joyous versions of our stories. This must become the pressing task of our scholars and practitioners. But the challenge facing Western secular humanism is, in my view, even more daunting – that of finding a story of any depth and vitality which is worth celebrating in the first place.

Whatever the narrative, there is still one more vital ingredient in all this that we neglect to our cost: truth has to be lived out – it has to be embodied – in flesh and blood, location and time. Perhaps, only then does it ever become truly believable or followable. Or, as a good friend of mine put it recently: 'Don't tell them what to do. Show them!'

Dying to belong

Having spent most of my life, one way or the other, both professionally as well as in a voluntary capacity, as a youth worker, I have constantly worked with young people in, or around, gangs.

Concern over, involvement in, and headlines about gang culture and its associated nihilism, misogyny and self-destructiveness are all on the increase around the world. In addition, the composition and nature of gang culture is shifting: gang members are getting younger, growing numbers of girls are getting involved, geographical territory is transcending drug territory, and violence is increasingly chaotic. The general increase in gang-related deaths of young people and, in particular, the number of high-profile murders is a constantly escalating problem.[109] Listen to some recent headlines from various cities around the world:

'Teen thugs kill noodle vendor.' Bangkok Post, 26 Jan 2015.[110]

'Teenage gang stabbed church minister's son and left him to die in the street.' Evening Standard, London, 30 March 2015.[111]

'Manenberg gang violence disrupts schools.' Eye Witness News, Cape Town, 15 May 2015.[112]

'He died in my hands': Bronx teen tried to save brother, 14, who was shot 16 times, in suspected gang.' May 23, 2015, New York Daily News.[113]

The *'Youth gangs, knife and gun crime'* bibliography, produced by The British Library, focuses on the causes for the rise and proliferation of youth gangs and responses in the UK, as well as by governments, police and schools, youth and social services in the USA, South Africa, France, Australia and New Zealand.[114] They are remarkably similar.

Opinion from criminologists, sociologists, and gang experts around the world is united. The rise of gang culture is closely linked to the breakdown of traditional community, along with the resultant absence of a sense of identity. *'While gangs may lead young people into dangerous situations and breed community division, distrust and fear, the friendship, support, security and sense of belonging they offer are often overlooked by those working with young people involved in gangs.'*[115] In other words, just like the issue of terrorism itself, the causes of gang violence are complex and will never be solved by enforcement alone.

Writing from a Latin American perspective, social psychologist Cordula Strocka explains that *'... while many causal factors need to be considered ... structural forces such as inequality and social exclusion largely account for the widespread rise in youth gang activity across Latin America since the 1990s.'*[116]

In the UK, gangs *'may form due to social exclusion and discrimination – people come together for a sense of safety and belonging. Immigrant populations, those excluded from education, or people who have engaged in criminal activities from an early age, are particularly at risk of gang involvement. Others may join a gang simply for something to do, seeking protection in numbers, or for reasons of status and peer pressure'* writes Kate Broadhurst, Head of Research with Perpetuity Research and Consultancy International at University of Leicester.[117]

Speaking again, within a UK context, the Executive Summary of the 2009 Centre for Social Justice Report, entitled poignantly *'Dying to Belong'*, explains: *'The modern gang is the product of the changing economic and social landscape of British society over the past few decades.'*

The report goes on to argue that the combination of youth unemployment and poor social housing becomes an incubator for social breakdown. The past few decades have witnessed an increasing socio-economic divide between the haves and the have-nots that, coupled with an environment of intense and overt consumerism, is often explicit in the global city where poverty and wealth sit side-by-side.

Alongside these socio-economic changes, the breakdown of the family unit has had a huge impact. The gang has become a substitute family with the gang leader as the 'father' for a significant number of young people growing up in our most deprived communities.

'These factors together have created, in certain communities, a generation of disenfranchised young people. Alienated from mainstream society these young people have created their own, alternative, society – the gang – and they live by the gang's rules: the 'code of the street'. As gangs have become more common over the past decade, territory has become increasingly important. For many gangs, defending geographical territory – often a post-code – has become part of their raison d'être, an integral part of their identity. This, together with the declining age of gang members, has contributed to the increasingly chaotic nature of gang violence.'[118]

But it's not just the socially excluded who are vulnerable. Louise Richardson argues that even though improving education would help to reduce extremism, it is clear – as we see from so many examples – that well-educated people were still capable of violent extremism. In fact, Richardson argues, *"The most combustible combination is an educated workforce and an economy that can't allow them to realise their expectations."*

We have to address these underlying socio-economic issues urgently. We can't dissociate terrorism from violent gangs or from the underlying issues of disenfranchisement by which they are driven.

The violent gang or the terrorist movement is a symptom of the problem, not the disease. Whilst, over the last years, the trend has been towards putting vast amounts of energy and resource into tackling the presenting issues, often the issues behind the issue, the cause or causes behind the behaviour, have been ignored.

Listening critically to the voices of gang members from around the world, in his book, 'A World of Gangs: Armed Young Men and Gangsta Culture', John Hagedorn, professor of criminal justice at the University of Illinois, Chicago, reaches three conclusions:

- Gangs are not a unique form, but one of many kinds of armed groups – including militia, terrorist cells, etc. – that occupy the uncontrolled spaces of a 'world of slums'.

- Understanding the cultural struggle for identity is crucial in working with gangs, which are shaped by racial and ethnic oppression, as well as poverty and slums, and are reactions of despair to persisting inequality.

- Nurturing a more life-affirming sense of identity, as a cultural counterforce to gang culture, creates changed behaviour.[119]

In 'Gangs, Marginalised Youth and Social Capital', Ross Deuchar agrees.[120] Based on research into the views of young people growing up in socially deprived urban areas of Glasgow, Scotland, he demonstrates that there is very clear and compelling evidence that many young people resist or move quickly out of gangs as soon as there are attractive alternatives to engage them such as sport and civic participation.[121]

I was radicalised at the age of 14. Through my attendance at a youth club at South Norwood Baptist Church in South London, my life was transformed. What changed it was the powerful combination of the investment of time into my life by young adults who I looked up to, and their teaching and example around the living out of the teaching of Jesus. I was inspired. Through this I was given the gift of a life-changing vision, a deep sense of purpose, and a feeling of belonging to a team. As I explain in '*Being Human*':

'I felt as though I was lifted out of the pettiness that had consumed so much of my energy to that point, and into a different dimension. As a result, I've slowly come to understand life in a particular way, which has brought shape, meaning and hope to my journey thus far. My small, flawed, personal, micro-story was given a bigger, global, even cosmic context as it was caught up into God's big story.' [122]

Good faith

The formation, and subsequent successes of the Civil Rights Movement in the USA, which became one of the most important political initiatives of the 20th century – challenges the conventional wisdom of both the political right and left about the relationship between faith, politics and positive social change. Not only does it demonstrate that faith is not necessarily politically conservative, but it also provided indisputable proof of the positive influence of faith on America's political life. Without religion, and Christianity in particular, it is not certain that the Civil Rights Movement would have taken place at all.

The hard work of the Civil Rights Movement – everything from organising rallies to bus boycotts – was achieved through the infrastructure of America's black churches. The words that inspired the movement were mostly the words of preachers, and King's own commitment to non-violent resistance – the bedrock of their success – was born out of and motivated by his faith. He constantly cited Jesus' command to *'love your enemies'* as one of the central guiding principles in his political life. The Civil Rights Movement, although as it grew it drew in a diversity of supporting groups, was rooted in churches and Christian morality and would, without doubt, in today's parlance, be known as a *'faith-based initiative.'*

This is the challenge. Perhaps rather than throwing the baby out with the bathwater, it is time to recognise the role that good faith plays in countless communities around the world. Although this might sound to some to be counter-intuitive, perhaps, in measure, it has been the West's very attempt to build secularist societies that is part of the problem we face. Good faith, which plays such a centring role in the lives of so many individuals and communities around the world – bringing a sense of rootedness and belonging – is often marginalised as irrelevant. To the extent that faith is excluded from the table, however, our society becomes more vacuous, our national conversation becomes more rudderless, our sense of purpose is lost, and a vacuum is left in which bad faith has the space to flourish and grow.

It is time to reclaim the term 'radical'.

The Latin word for 'root' is *radix*, from which was derived *radicalis* meaning 'forming the root' or 'being rooted'. Slowly, the term 'radical' also began to be applied to people who were committed to bringing about far-reaching and thorough – 'root and branch' – change relating to the fundamental nature of something. And at the age of 14, that was me. I felt that I'd been caught up in a radical vision to bring positive change to the world. Put differently, I joined a gang – a gang that was worth belonging to! I stepped into a narrative that was worth dedicating my life to.[123]

It is time get radical!

TEN
A Tale of Two Pathways

A man stands on a stage in Lynchburg, Virginia.

His audience is a basketball arena full of 18 – 22-year-old students, at Liberty University. The school prides itself on being the largest private, non-profit university in the USA, the largest university in Virginia, and the largest Christian university in the world. It is certainly one of the most influential evangelical centres in America.

It is December 2015, and a few days beforehand, 14 people have died in an act of Islamic terrorism perpetrated by a 28-year-old man and his 29-year-old wife, in San Bernardino, California.

Jerry Falwell Jr., is the president of Liberty University, and the son of its founder, the late religious right leader, Jerry Falwell Sr. To a crammed hall he thunders:

"It just blows my mind that the president of the United States [says] that the answer to circumstances like that is more gun control."

The students burst into applause.

"If some of those people in that community centre had what I have in my back pocket right now ...," he continues whilst being interrupted by louder cheers and clapping. *"Is it illegal to pull it out? I don't know,"* he says, chuckling.

"I've always thought that if more good people had concealed-carry permits, then we could end those Muslims before they walked in."

"I just wanted to take this opportunity to encourage all of you to get your permit. We offer a free course. Let's teach them a lesson if they ever show up here."

Following his comments, Falwell retweeted several tweets praising his remarks, including one that said, *"SUCK IT, Muslim extremists,"* with a link to the weapons course Liberty University offers.[124]

Another time, another country

A packed theatre of predominantly Asian men mumble to themselves, chattering to each other in anticipation of what this small Indian man is about to tell them.

A handful of white officials and policemen sit anxiously on the front row, uncertain that this meeting will pass off peacefully.

In 1893, a young Gandhi, yet to become the famed liberator of India, arrived in South Africa and found himself thrown into the furnace that was to refine his thinking and define his destiny. He was shocked and traumatised by the open discrimination and oppression of coloured and black people by the white minority there, which in the first years of the 1900s grew even more intrusive as it was enshrined in the form of new legislation. So it was that the young lawyer found himself addressing a meeting to put in place a plan of action to undermine the government and subvert the repressive law. He hushes the assembled crowd and begins to speak.

"General Smuts' new law states that a policeman, passing an Indian dwelling, may enter and demand the identity card of any Indian woman whose dwelling it is. Understand, he does not have to stand at the door. He may enter."

An explosion of disbelief erupts in the theatre and angry men shout out a barrage of responses. *"I swear that I will kill the man who offers that insult to my home and my wife." "Talk means nothing. Kill a few officials before they disgrace one Indian woman. Then they might think twice about such laws." "For that cause I would be willing to die."*

Gandhi waves his hands to try to calm the volatile situation and the men sit once more to hear what he has to say.

"I praise such courage. I need such courage because in this cause I too am prepared to die. But my friends, there is no cause for which I am prepared to kill. Whatever they do to us we will attack no one. Kill no one. But we will not give our fingerprints. Not one of us. They will imprison us, they will fine us and they will seize our possessions. But they cannot take away our self-respect if we

do not give it to them. I am asking you to fight – to fight against their anger, not to provoke it. We will not strike a blow. But we will receive them. And through our pain we will make them see their injustice. And it will hurt, as all fighting hurts. But we cannot lose. We cannot. They may torture my body. Break my bones. Even kill me. Then they will have my dead body. Not my obedience ... Let us take a solemn oath, that come what may, we will not submit to this law."

Silence descends on the theatre. Then, one by one, starting with a withered old man, those gathered begin to stand as a declaration that they will follow Gandhi in his non-violent overthrow of apartheid.[125]

The contrast between the words of Jerry Falwell Jr. and those of Gandhi – two men of huge influence – could not be greater.

Mohandas Karamchand Gandhi's story is an extraordinary testament to just how much a real and solid commitment to non-violence can achieve. Not only did Gandhi, the 'little man', live to see independence granted to his beloved home country of India, but he also helped set in motion the beginning of the movement that eventually led to the peaceful downfall of apartheid in South Africa. Added to that, he provided the inspiration for Martin Luther King in his successful campaign to abolish the racist laws of the southern states of North America; a genuinely remarkable achievement for any leader, especially for one who never held political office or military command.

But equally astonishing is that, although much of his non-violent stance was self-consciously based on his understanding of the example of Jesus, together with teaching from Hinduism, Buddhism, Jainism and Sikhism, who all share the idea of nonviolence (*ahimsa*), he never embraced Christianity. Mahatma – or the 'Great Soul', as he came to be known – saw the Church and the West in general as unwilling to follow Jesus' teaching truly in this area. Perhaps, as a result, although he was always proud to talk openly about his deep commitment to the example of Jesus, he was equally keen to avoid any association with Christianity or the Church.

The first Christmas after September 11th, I interviewed a well-known American pastor and theologian for a network breakfast television show in the UK. It was Christmas Day, so I invited him to come into the studio to talk about the Christian message and how we could apply it to the world in which we live. I opened by asking him what Christmas was about for him.

"Christmas is about peace and goodwill to all," he replied, *"Jesus is the Prince of Peace. If we close ourselves off from this message then it can't make a difference."*

"So if Jesus is the Prince of Peace and one of his key messages was love your enemies, what does that mean on a world scale?" I asked. *"How should it affect American foreign policy? What is your message to world leaders this Christmas?"*

"I think it's easier to understand Jesus' message on a person-to-person level – it doesn't necessarily apply to nation/state relationships," was his short reply.

After the show I asked one of the studio crew what he thought of what our Reverend guest had said. His reply was simple, *"Love your enemy, but kill them first!"*

A just war?

The American pastor's words actually spoke of his commitment to a 'Just War' theory, which is based around the view that whilst war is always terrible, as a last resort, it is not always the worst option. There may be responsibilities so important, outcomes so undesirable or potential atrocities so horrific, that they justify a carefully planned and justly fought military intervention.

For several centuries, the Church was known for its stance against violence as a tool to achieve either personal or nationalistic aims. Rather than an inactive pacifism, this sprang from an understanding that Jesus' teaching called for a different way of actively taking on 'the enemy', but doing so non-violently. However, two events were to change all this:

In the 4th century, the Emperor Constantine declared that the Roman Empire was officially Christian. This caused a huge clash of worldviews. How could such a dominant cultural and political force disband its armies when it had been built on, and was sustained by, military strength?

Then, in the following century, the influential Christian leader, Augustine of Hippo – a child of Greek thinking and Roman life – created a theology to fit the reality of the empire in which he lived.[126] Augustine argued for the separation of Jesus' teaching into personal and national ideals. He recognised that Jesus called for non-violence from Christians at a personal level and that they *'should not take up the sword in self-defence'*. He believed that the principle of love, however, also constrained Christians to defend their neighbours – and that in that defence, violence might be necessary. God, he taught, had given the sword to government for good reason. Indeed, to offer no armed resistance in the face of a grave wrong, which could not be avoided in any other way, would be a sin. A Christian could therefore be a soldier and, in this way, serve both God and country honourably.[127]

So it was that Augustine sowed the first seeds of modern Just War military ethics, which Thomas Aquinas – another immensely influential philosopher and Christian theologian – was to develop further and popularise in the 13th century by laying out the conditions under which a war could be declared as just.

Over the last centuries, this doctrine of Just War has, in turn, become the study not only of theologians and ethicists, but of countless politicians, policy makers and military leaders as the criteria have developed around two sets of questions concerning the right to go to war (is it a just cause?) and the right conduct in war (is it fought in a just way?). In recent years, a growing number of theorists have also proposed a third category of questions centring around ensuring justice after armed intervention, including looking at responsibilities around peace treaties, war crimes, trials, compensations and credible strategies for reconstruction.

Likewise, an array of theological schools across the diversity of the Muslim community have developed similar, albeit simpler, versions of this same kind of thinking. These are used to justify military intervention as a result of the threat or reality of the mistreatment or oppression of a Muslim community, or treaty breaking.

Whatever the rationale, the arguments are well understood. There are some forces so evil that if not restrained by force, will impose themselves on innocent people the world over. What of Hitler's Germany and his attempt to wipe out the Jewish race? What of ISIS and the wider threat from Islamic terrorists? When our enemy is not open to negotiation; when all attempts at dialogue have proven unsuccessful, what do we do? Is it not simply irresponsible to rule out armed intervention, when all else has failed?

The problem is that the concept and practice of Just War raises as many questions as it does answers. And these lie in two main areas.

The first is philosophical and has to do with the problem of subjectivity. If a Just War can only be fought for a good and just cause rather than for self-gain or as an exercise of power, this opens up a hornet's nest of questions around legitimacy, which have only been complicated in recent years by the erosion of trust in the statements and promises of politicians in the UK, America and elsewhere.

The second, however, is very practical. Does war work? Is the ultimate weakness of violence that it creates and sustains a descending spiral; begetting constantly the very thing it seeks to destroy? Perhaps violence can never stop violence, simply because every 'successful' violent act deepens our faith in it and this very success leads others to imitate it. So, like a contagious disease it spreads and blights our whole world. Gandhi wrote: *'I object to violence because when it appears to do good, the good is only temporary; the evil it does is permanent.'*

When Jesus first announced that one of the central distinctives of his new agenda – or gospel – for life was to *'love your enemies'*, he could not have made a more controversial statement.[128] At the time, Israel was under Roman rule and its occupying forces universally hated, but groups such as the Zealots (the 'Dagger Men'), with their talk of bloody revolution, had caught the imagination of the Jewish people. Violent overthrow seemed not only the most obvious solution to rid the land of 'the evil empire', but also the only solution. This is what the contemporary American Christian theologian, Walter Wink describes as *'the myth of redemptive violence'*; the belief that liberation, strength, protection and sustained freedom can only come from the power that violence gives to a person or a nation.

Jesus' advice about non-violence is still viewed as impractical idealism that would never work in practice, although extraordinarily, no such charge is ever made against violence, in spite of the fact that history has proved, time and again, that guns and planes, wars and smart bombs solve little in the long run.

When the US tried to bomb North Vietnam and Cambodia into submission, not only did their efforts fail, at great cost in both human and financial terms, but their intervention also gave rise to the dictatorship of Pol Pot and the deaths through executions, malnutrition and poor medical care of an estimated 25 per cent of the Cambodian population.[129]

The consequences of the Western allies bombing Iraq, in order to remove Saddam Hussein, have been horrific and are ongoing to this very day. Likewise, Israeli and Palestinian forces seem to be bound together in an endless cycle of violence and retaliation.

Our experience teaches us that whenever aggression is met with aggression, the beast of violence is fed and grows stronger. *'Whoever opts for revenge'*, says the Chinese proverb, *'should dig two graves'*. Put differently, our bombs may wipe out the warriors of ISIS, but their sons, daughters and grandchildren have very long memories. It is a sobering point that, as the Bible teaches, one generation always inherits the consequences of the sins of their forefathers.[130] The further down the pipe of power and violence we allow ourselves to slide, the harder it is to stop and find a way to climb out. It is far easier just to keep on sliding.[131]

Even the perennial chestnut around what else, if anything, could the world have done about Hitler's Germany, forgets the impact of the legacy of the Treaty of Versailles. Was John Maynard Keynes, right? Did it amount to *'one of the most serious acts of political unwisdom for which our statesmen have ever been responsible'*? What was its impact on the development of German politics in the 1920s and 1930s? Did it almost inevitably lead to the outbreak of World War II?

It was the American author Jim Wallis who once pointed out that Jesus' famous words *'Love your enemies'* probably amount to, at one and the same time, the most admired and least practised piece of teaching in history. Despite the claim that many of Western civilisation's roots are to be found in the Christian faith, and the fact that there is almost universal admiration and respect for leaders such as Gandhi, Martin Luther King, Rosa Parks, Desmond Tutu, or the older Nelson Mandela, who lived out this 'upside down' non-violent ethical approach to life, the myth that violence is the only solution to many of the world's problems still thrives.

Muscle, punching-power, and military strength create and sustain stability, we are told. But, have we actually been deluded into believing a myth that is destroying us? As Bono once sang in U2's song *Peace on Earth*, *'Who said that if you go in hard you won't get hurt?'* Or, in Jesus' words, *'For all who draw the sword will die by the sword.'*[132]

Whilst it is undeniable that the teaching of the Qur'an is not as developed around the theme of non-violence and reconciliation as that of Jesus, as Dave Andrews sobering words remind us, *'There have been more devastating wars among Christian states fighting each other than between Christian and Muslim states; and predominantly Christian states have killed more Jews and Muslims than predominantly Muslim states have killed Christians or Jews.'*[133]

But despite its chequered performance, Christianity remains a religion of peace. That's the very essence of the man we know as Jesus who came to preach the gospel – or good news – of peace, and died for his peaceful, subversive teachings at the hands of an empire and religious structure hell-bent on so-called redemptive violence.[134]

In just the same way, however flawed the practice of Islam, in essence, it is a religion of peace. Indeed, that is the very heart of the term itself, which is derived from the Arabic root 'Salema' meaning peace, purity, submission and obedience.

So, to quote Qur'an 5.32, which is widely held across the Muslim community as the foundation for creating a movement committed to the centrality of finding non-violent approaches to conflict resolution, both within and beyond the Ummah:

'Whoever slays a person, it is as if he had slain mankind entirely ... and whosoever gives life to a soul, it shall be as if he had given life to mankind altogether.'

Or, to quote Qur'an Verse 5:48, with its mandate to all peoples of the Book (Jews, Christians and Muslims):

'We have appointed a law and a practice for every one of you. Had God willed, He would have made you a single community, but He wanted to test you regarding what has come to you. So compete with each other in doing good. Every one of you will return to God and He will inform you regarding the things about which you differed.'

Jew, Christian, Muslim, Sikh, Hindu or Atheist; we are always imprisoned by our exclusion of those who are different to us, never released by it. It is only as we build bridges with those who don't see life our way that we begin to confront and deal with the hidden and ugly parts of our own beliefs and culture and begin to find the pathway to peace.

Do governments, guns and traditional armies have a role to play in our war against the worst forms of terrorism? Perhaps. But, can they win the peace? No. In this they are impotent. Instead, we must find a new narrative to live by together. Real change comes from the periphery. It arises from local communities, one relationship at a time. Every act of love is a victory over hatred. Every act of kindness is a victory over violence. There is no other way.

As Muslim scholars work to reclaim the word 'jihad' from the violent extremists who have misappropriated it, and endeavour to reframe it as a 'radical, practical, non-violent, sacred struggle for justice', can the West re-evaluate Jesus' example and teaching – one of the most important prophets in the Islamic tradition – the ideal, interfaith, role model to bring Muslims and Christians together to work for that non-violent jihad?[135]

The Qur'an, of course, considers Jesus, (*Isa*), not only a great prophet but also the Messiah (al-*Masih*) – which literally means 'anointed one' or 'liberator' – sent to guide the God's people with new scripture, *al-Injjl* (the gospel).[136]

In Islamic theology, Jesus is the only prophet or messenger of the end times and, like all the prophets, is considered a Muslim (one who submits to the will of God). The Qur'an also teaches that Isa is alive in heaven and it is he who will return to earth, near the Last Day, to restore justice and to defeat *al-Masih ad-Dajjal* (the false liberator or messiah).[137]

Isa's final task – according to both Sunni and Shia Muslims – will be to assist the al-*Mahdi* (the guided one) in this task of overcoming the 'false Messiah' and then in unifying the

Muslim *Ummah* under the common purpose of the pure worship of Allah – thereby ending divisions and deviations.[138]

As we move forward, our different cultures and religions will either continue to feed the old '*clash of civilisations*' narrative or – if we can get back to the real fundamentals, the narrative of our common humanity – it will become the central and indispensable resource in the battle to overcome inter-communal conflict and win the lasting peace. The choice is ours.

What does all this mean for our current situation, nationally, internationally and globally? What does it mean for the way we wage our war on terrorism or fight for peace? What should we be promoting in order to build that elusive sense of cohesion? What kind of *counter-narrative* do we need on which to build a *counter-extremist strategy* that is powerful enough not only to reverse the present trend but more than that, to bring real peace to our vulnerable multi-faith, multi-cultural communities and to our wider world?

Martin Luther King once said, *"If humanity is to progress, Gandhi is inescapable. He lived, thought and acted, inspired by the vision of humanity evolving toward world peace. We ignore him at our own risk."*

Perhaps the world – Western, Christian, Islamic and Jewish – would do well to invite Gandhi, the 'little man' of Hinduism, and his creativity back into the conversation.

ELEVEN
Winning the Peace

On Saturday 21st September 2013, a group of unidentified gunmen mounted an attack on the upmarket Westgate shopping mall in Nairobi, Kenya, leaving 67 dead and another 175 wounded. As the world struggled to absorb the brutality behind the headlines they were reading, al-Shabaab, the extremist Islamic group based in Somalia, claimed responsibility in retaliation for the Kenyan military's support of the Somali government.[139]

Just under a year later, however, the news was different. On 1st September 2014, a US drone strike killed al-Shabaab's leader, Moktar Ali Zubeyr. Political analysts immediately hailed the insurgent commander's death as a major symbolic and operational loss for the terrorist group and suggested its impact would lead to the group's fragmentation and dissolution. Indeed, in line with these predictions, in January 2015, the UN was able to report that the militant group was shrinking and on the retreat.[140]

This rhetoric, however, was proven all too hollow when, on 2nd April 2015, masked al-Shabaab militants, heavily armed and strapped with explosives, stormed the campus of Garissa University College in Eastern Kenya, massacring 148 people in cold blood and injuring at least another 79. The gunmen had taken over 700 students hostage, choosing to free

Muslims (those who could recite the Qur'an) and kill those who couldn't or who identified as Christians. The attack was the deadliest Kenya had seen in over two decades.

This *'war on terrorism'* is a new kind of war; a war that cannot be won by governments, guns, planes, drones and traditional armies, however sophisticated they are.

If the task is to stop terrorist groups being able to groom and brainwash a constant supply of new recruits, to deal with the failures of integration which leaves some young people vulnerable to the *'glamour'* of joining up and to build stronger, more resilient, more cohesive communities, we have to find a different way of going about it.

And, as gang members get younger, the violence on the streets of our cities increases, our detention centres and prisons fill to capacity and the rate of recidivism escalates, we would be fools if we did not ask ourselves whether we are travelling on the right road.

Perhaps the key to combatting the problems of exclusion and the threat of extremism is the same.

Our determination to win this war, or rather to win 'this peace', must be relentless, for the price of failure is huge. *'If we are serious about peace, then we must work as ardently, seriously, continuously, carefully and bravely as we have ever prepared for war'*, commented American author, Wendell

Berry, in his 2003 book '*Citizenship Papers*'. That means we just can't afford to pin our hopes on the possibility that somehow current policies and approaches will miraculously produce new outcomes that, so far, they have failed to deliver. Instead, it is time to invest in developing and deploying new approaches that address the identity crisis that many young people feel, by working to bring our communities together and extend opportunity to all.

To return to the questions posed at the very beginning of this book; how do we protect young people from being vulnerable to the propaganda of those who seek to perpetuate violence? What can we do to provide alternative, positive role models to a generation of disenfranchised young people? What do effective counter-exclusion and counter-extremism strategies actually look like? What should we be promoting, rather than simply working to prevent, in order to build that elusive sense of cohesion?

I am convinced that we can only defeat the narratives of exclusion, extremism and terrorism by offering a new, positive, healthy and compelling narrative that is worth living by; a narrative that builds bridges of peace, relationship-by-relationship; a narrative that is owned at grass-roots level by local communities.

In order to do that, we have to find new ways of tackling the issue of integration – ensuring that young people enjoy meaningful contact and then relationships with those from other cultural backgrounds and faiths. We need to deploy strategies and projects designed to end the segregation and marginalisation that is still all too evident in our society, as well as to create a new sense of inclusion, shared belonging, ownership and understanding.

National governments have an indispensable and central role to play in all this. If we want lasting peace, domestic socio-economic divisions, Western foreign policies and the unequal distribution of the 'goods' of globalisation must all be, as we have seen, challenged and rethought.

Equally important, however, is the work of individuals and local communities. Every individual has a vital role because 'social capital' is, in the end, built one relationship at a time. At the same time, it is the task of all those entrusted with community leadership to work to create the environment in which these connections are more likely to develop. In the end, only this is capable of offering a counter, to what will otherwise be the continuing fragmentation of communities.

Inspired to inspire

In early August 2011, Mark Duggan, a 29-year-old Tottenham resident, was shot and killed by police whilst sitting in the back seat of a car. The circumstances of his death sparked riots not only in his local community, but also across London and then around the UK in the following days. Many ordinary young people were caught up in the rioting as an ugly 'herd' mentality took over.

The situation became so serious that, a week later, on Thursday 11th August, Parliament was recalled to debate the situation. By then, however, the violence had subsided and the damage had been done. According to the press, more than 48,000 local businesses had suffered financial loss as a result of the looting and rioting.

Two days earlier, on Tuesday 9th August, my phone rang. It was a call from a senior officer of one of the local authorities where Oasis runs a secondary school.

The gist of the conversation went like this. The night before, as rioting and looting spread across London, a building very near to our school had been torched by a gang of around 20 young rioters. Eight fire engines and 40 fire-fighters had tackled the blaze, to no avail. The building collapsed and burned to the ground.

The point of the call was not primarily to inform me of these events, but to warn me that 'intelligence' had been received by police about the evening ahead, which indicated that the gang who had burned down that building were planning the same for our academy that night.

I asked what I could do. *"Nothing,"* came the reply. All police leave across London had been cancelled and extra police had been drafted in from across the country. But with widespread rioting, the police policy was that they would only deploy officers to respond to situations that had already developed.

"They just can't protect every building," I was told. *"So I'm ringing to advise you to ensure that the Oasis building is locked down securely and that no staff are on or around the site, which would only jeopardise their safety. If the building is attacked, the police and fire brigade will attend, but the priority tonight is to protect lives – the emergency services don't have the capacity to guard public buildings."*

The call over, I stood and thought. What could I do? I decided to make two calls.

I rang a senior member of our finance team and asked them to talk with our insurance and security companies. I wanted to ensure that no night-security personnel were put in danger. It was also essential to inform our insurers of what we knew about the situation. But I knew that although this call would help with damage limitation – it wouldn't save the building. For that I had to make another call to our local youth team.

It was 4.45pm when I made the second call. I got straight to the point. I told them what I knew. I didn't need to explain the devastating impact that the destruction of our brand-new academy building would have, for our students, the whole community and for the whole nation.

But here's the truth; our school building didn't burn. Why? Because, besides anything else, one of our youth workers is a great baker, and she and her team – mostly volunteers, including some of the older young people they worked with – armed only with a huge number of delicious cakes, sat and talked with all those out on the streets that evening, bringing peace to what might otherwise have been a very difficult scenario.

It was a late night – but it passed peacefully because our team were able to 'trade' on the depth of relationships in which they had invested over the years beforehand. When it really counted, it was this that made the critical difference and which changed history, for the better, for everyone.

As Eleanor Roosevelt, the diplomat, human rights activist and wife of Franklin, who served as American President through the period of the Second War World, once said: *"It isn't enough to talk about peace. One must believe in it. And it isn't enough to believe in it. One must work at it."*

Inspired

Globally, it is imperative that we develop a plethora of imaginative new approaches to the task of combatting terror and building lasting peace. If the first years of this millennium have taught us anything, it must be that all the current strategies have to offer us is damage limitation – but even that is debatable!

Using the UK's PREVENT strategy as an example, whilst nobody would want to disagree with its goals, if we really want to succeed rather than simply attempting to 'prevent', we must also learn how to 'inspire'; inspire young people by giving them a compelling overarching story to live by that adds value to the world by bringing peace, at the same time as it brings them to a deeper and more compelling sense of self-worth, purpose and direction.[141]

What does it mean to work at peace? How do we enable young people to develop the core skills around active listening, negotiation and dialogue, conflict resolution, community building and social responsibility, as well as a respect for and celebration of diversity of religion and culture?

So, at this point, a short pause for another word of explanation. Whilst the ideas that follow are specifically designed for use in the UK, I am convinced that, although the practicalities need to be thought through country by country, the core principles which sit behind them are capable of cultural adaptation and application for many different national contexts. Take them and use them – and if we can help, get in touch.

Responding to Eleanor Roosevelt's challenge for action rather than words, at Oasis we are looking to do our bit, through INSPIRE.

INSPIRE is a peacemaking initiative designed to support young people in finding a positive narrative for their lives; a sense of worth, direction and belonging which will enable them to live fulfilling, peaceful lives where they aren't vulnerable to the lure of gangs, violence, extremism and terror.

INSPIRE is a call to action for schools, youth workers and young people across the UK and beyond to take positive action to contribute to building peace – between neighbours, amongst friends and families – both in our local communities and across the wider world.

INSPIRE is a mechanism to implement the intent of the PREVENT strategy, and government's wider goal of achieving greater integration, for young people, in an accessible, meaningful and inspiring way.

INSPIRE is designed to add value to the educational curriculum, as well as to support this through extra-curricular activities that have peacemaking at their core.

Launched with the publication of this book, INSPIRE will, over the coming years, enable young people to develop practical peacemaking skills, encourage and enthuse them to use those skills proactively within their local communities and give them the opportunity to celebrate their role in building bridges of peace for the future.

INSPIRE is designed to create the opportunity for a generation of young people to:

- Think about the needs of the whole world from an integrated global perspective.

- Recognise that every life has value.

- Ask themselves what kind of person they want to become.

- Live the best version of their story.

- Become active peacemakers.

How will INSPIRE work?

On 11th November 2018, we will commemorate the centenary of the signing of the Armistice, which brought an end to the First World War – the war they said would *'end all wars'*. We are looking to seize that moment, which will bring the issues and questions around conflict and peacemaking to the top of the agenda.

Just 21 years after the *'Great War'* had ended, the world was at war again and, indeed, throughout the 100 years since, has continued to be ravaged by violent conflict, discord and enmity.

So, the centenary of the end of the First World War offers more than the opportunity for collective acts of remembrance. It also creates the opportunity to commemorate, celebrate and to question. Why didn't the 'peace' of 1918 hold? What was the impact of its failure? What can we learn in order to create lasting peace in our communities? What are the principles of peace building? How can we truly honour those who fought and died for others in the First World War and in subsequent wars and conflicts? Why is that important? What are the skills we need? How do we develop them?

INSPIRE is made up of three core components, which I believe have the power to inspire a generation of peacemakers.

1. CURRICULUM DEVELOPMENT

It is time to put peacemaking more centrally on the curriculum of every school in a very explicit way. The consequences of an education that develops intellectual competency without an equal emphasis on character alongside active community participation are all too evident in our world today. Only this broad approach to education can inspire and equip young people for life in community.

The INSPIRE peace curriculum focuses on:

- Encouraging young people to explore and debate current world issues in a safe environment.

- Creating awareness and understanding of the causes of conflict, whether within friendship and family groups or between cultures and nations.

- Teaching young people to question assumptions that they have been taught as fact.

- Facilitating a sense of belonging, not only within the school community, but also within wider local and global communities.

2. 1000 DAYS OF PEACE

The 1000-day period between February 2016 and Armistice Day 2018 offers a unique opportunity both in the UK and some other countries.

In 2012, in celebration of London hosting the Olympics, Oasis, the charity that I founded and work for, launched 100 Days of Peacemaking, an initiative aimed at celebrating the age-old tradition of keeping peace 50 days before and 50 days after the Olympics and highlighting our commitment to build stronger, more peaceful communities.

Now '1000 Days of Peace' will build on that experience and offer schools and young people across the UK, and beyond, a variety of national projects to get involved in. We've created a whole set of resources for schools and youth groups to help them to identify areas of conflict within their community and inspire them to create projects in response to those conflict areas. These include, amongst several others:

- **Kicking off peace**
  Sport always offers an excellent opportunity to teach young people of all ages a wide variety of necessary life skills and values. Using 'football3' (an established peace-building tool), we will be 'kicking off peace' in the playground with a series of annual tournaments, bringing children from different schools together in games played without referees. 'football3' requires players to learn how to resolve conflicts themselves through dialogue and compromise, with the

support of specially trained mediators from more senior years, as well as other community organisations.

- **A Peace of Art**

  A Peace of Art is a nationwide competition that will give young people the opportunity to design and install public artwork within their local community. A series of especially developed lesson plans help teachers, children's and youth workers, encourage young people to explore the meaning of peace, at an individual, family, community, national and international level, whilst a detailed project brief is available to advise on practical details including size, materials and budget.

  The entries for A Peace of Art will be judged by a panel of nationally and internationally renowned artists, and the 100 winning designs – one for every year since the end of the First World War – will be curated as an exhibition through 2018. All the completed artworks will be unveiled and used as part of the national Peace 2018 celebrations in November 2018.

- **Anthem for Peace**

  Written by young people to be sung by young people, this anthem will be a collaborative work, coordinated by a nationally known musician. It will also form a focal point of our Peace 2018 events in November 2018, when it will be sung simultaneously by young people around the UK,

their voices united in calling for a peaceful world for themselves and future generations.

- **Growing Peace**

  Planning, creating and caring for a Peace Garden is a great
  way of bringing communities together. As well as providing
  a nurturing and healing space for the enjoyment of all, they
  also serve as an outdoor environment in which children
  can learn how to care for the earth and each other. Our aim
  is to inspire the development of 100 Peace Gardens across
  the UK by November 2018.

- **Young Peacemakers**

  Our Young Peacemakers initiative will see children and
  young people across the UK commit themselves to
  actively demonstrating peacemaking behaviour through
  community engagement and activity. Teachers, children's
  and youth workers, will regularly seek to recognise young
  peacemakers, with the ultimate reward being a Peacemakers
  Button, presented annually, and which unlocks rewards for
  both the individual and the school or project.

3. PEACE 2018

The projects and initiatives of the 1000 Days of Peace campaign
will culminate in Peace 2018; a series of simultaneous events
of remembrance and hope, which will take place across the
UK on Friday 9th November 2018 in town and community
halls, cathedrals and mosques, synagogues, churches and
temples, as well as war memorials around the country. Peace

2018 will offer young people from every school across the UK the opportunity to be part a poignant and inspiring event; an interactive and engaging way of participating in this nationally significant anniversary, bringing communities together and enabling them to commit themselves to a peaceful future.

And just like 1000 Days of Peace, Peace 2018 will be built on a pilot event which Oasis delivered, in November 2014, when we worked with a group of twenty schools in Lambeth and Southwark in South London, as well as the Imperial War Museum, a partnership of local churches and other faith groups and the two local authorities, to bring over 900 young people together in an act of collective remembrance to pay tribute to those who fought and died in the First World War, and to commit to be active peacemakers in their local communities.

Peace 2018 will be supported by a suite of specially developed teaching resources, created by Oasis and the Imperial War Museum, working with a number of other national and global other partners.

It is time to get radical.

INSPIRE
Peacemaking for young people

For schools, children's and youth groups across the UK and beyond

INSPIRE is designed to support young people in finding a positive narrative for their lives; a sense of worth, direction and belonging, to enable them to live fulfilling, peaceful lives where they aren't vulnerable to the lure of gangs, violence, extremism and terror.

To find out more and to keep up to date with information about the project, visit **oasisuk.org/inspire** or contact us via any of the below:

020 7921 4200
inspire@oasisuk.org

@1000daysofpeace

www.facebook.com/1000daysofpeace

TWELVE:
Digging Deeper
(For everyone who wants
to know a little more)

1   On August 7th, 1998, al-Qaeda struck the US embassies in Kenya and
     Tanzania, killing 224 people, including 12 Americans. In retaliation,
     President Bill Clinton launched *Operation Infinite Reach*, a bombing
     campaign in Sudan and Afghanistan against targets that the US asserted
     were associated with al-Qaeda. Many have since questioned whether
     or not a giant pharmaceutical plant – which produced much of the
     region's antimalarial drugs and around 50 per cent of Sudan's pharma-
     ceutical needs – that the Americans chose to bomb, was ever used as a
     chemical warfare plant. The strikes failed to kill any leaders of either
     al-Qaeda or the Taliban. Two years later came al-Qaeda's attempted
     bombing of Los Angeles International Airport, and on October 12th,
     2000, the bombing of the guided-missile destroyer USS *Cole* while it
     was harboured in the Yemeni port of Aden, which killed 17 US Navy
     sailors and left another 39 injured.

2   Tony Blair, *We need to challenge the Jihadi narrative.* Speech at National
     9/11 Memorial & Museum, New York. Tuesday, Oct 6th, 2015.

3   Retrieved from *The Reunion: Guantanamo Bay.* Radio 4. First broad-
     cast 16th August 2015.

4   Figures from *Costs of War*, a study by Brown University's Watson
     Institute for International Studies, published in 2015, which looked
     at war-related deaths, injuries and displacement in Afghanistan and
     Pakistan from 2001 to 2014, when international combat troops left
     Afghanistan. The study is also supported by UN figures, which show
     that in Afghanistan, civilian casualties rose 16 per cent in the first four
     months of 2015, with 974 people killed and a further 1,963 wounded.
     Whilst military deaths are logged with precision, Neta Crawford, the
     report's author, explains civilian figures are difficult to source, but

that they are based on statistics from the United Nations Assistance Mission in Afghanistan, as well as other sources.

5   The Bush Administration based the invasion of Iraq in 2003 principally on the assertion that Saddam Hussein's government possessed weapons of mass destruction (WMDs) and therefore posed an immediate threat to the United States and its coalition allies. Saddam was also accused of harbouring and supporting al-Qaeda.

The invasion began on 20th March, when America, joined by the United Kingdom and several coalition allies, launched a '*shock and awe*' surprise attack without declaring war. Iraqi forces were quickly overwhelmed, the Ba'athist government collapsed, and Saddam was captured (in December) and executed by a military court three years later.

The power vacuum following Saddam's demise, combined with the mismanagement of the occupation, led to widespread sectarian violence between Shias and Sunnis, as well as a lengthy insurgency against US and coalition forces.

From the start of the War on Terror in 2001, Tony Blair supported the foreign policy of George W. Bush. As a result, the UK participated in the 2001 invasion of Afghanistan as well as that of Iraq. The UK's rationale for involvement in the 2003 invasion was that Iraq could deploy weapons of mass destruction '*within 45 minutes of an order to use them.*' After the invasion, however, no substantial evidence was found to verify the initial claims about WMDs and the rationale for, and misrepresentation of, pre-war intelligence continues to face heavy criticism both domestically and internationally.

The US began withdrawing its troops from Iraq in the winter of 2007–2008, a winding down which accelerated under President Barack Obama. The last remaining UK combat troops were withdrawn in July 2009, whereas the US formally withdrew all its combat troops from Iraq at the end of 2011.

6   Based on figures and information from Wikipedia's 'List of terrorist incidents, 2015'.

7   The Islamic State (IS) was born in post-war Iraq, it grew in the wake of
     conflict in Syria, and it is expanding in places like Libya. It is known in
     Arabic as ad-Dawlah al-Islāmiyah fī 'l-'Irāq wa-sh-Shām, leading to the
     acronym Da'ish, Da'eesh, or DAESH, the Arabic equivalent of ISIL.

8   On 29th June 2014, ISIL proclaimed itself to be a worldwide cali-
     phate, with Abu Bakr al-Baghdadi being named its caliph and, as part
     of this, renamed itself 'Islamic State'. As a caliphate, it claims religious,
     political and military authority over all Muslims worldwide, and that
     '*the legality of all emirates, groups, states, and organisations, becomes null
     by the expansion of the khilāfah's [caliphate's] authority and arrival of its
     troops to their areas*'. (From *Abu Bakr al-Baghdadi: The man who would
     be caliph*. The Week. 13th September 2014). A caliphate is a form
     of Islamic political-religious leadership centring around a caliph – or
     'successor' – to Muhammad.

     For a fascinating and insightful article on how ISIS developed see:
     The Terror Strategist: Secret Files Reveal the Structure of Islamic State by
     Christoph Reuter.

     http://www.spiegel.de/international/world/islamic-state-files-show-
     structure-of-islamist-terror-group-a-1029274.html

9   Emman El-Badawy, Milo Comerford and Peter Welby, *Inside the
     Jihadi Mind: Understanding Ideology and Propaganda*. The Centre on
     Religion & Geopolitics, Oct 2015.

10   Reported in The Week, *What is Salafism and should we be worried by it?*
     Jan 19th, 2015.

     Salafism takes its name from the Arabic term salaf ('predecessors',
     'ancestors'). The Salafi movement is an ultra-conservative orthodox
     branch of Sunni Islam. It rejects religious innovation (bida) and looks
     to recreate society as it was run in the 7th century. However, Salafism
     encompasses a huge range of beliefs – extending from, non-political,
     non-violent religious devotion on one hand, to violent extremism on
     the other.

Most Sunni leaders consider the militant form of Salafism (Salafi jihadism), often referred to as Wahhabism (following the teaching of the 18th century scholar Muhammed bin 'Abd al-Wahhab), as beyond the fold of Sunni Islam and that, rather than adhering to the fundamental tenets of Islam, it represents instead, what they regard as apostasy. Al-Wahhab evangelised the Arabian Peninsula in a call to return to the practices of the early Muslims. His followers see themselves as an Islamic 'reform movement' dedicated to restoring 'pure monotheistic worship', believing that modern imperialist corruption is destroying the world.

Although the whole Salafi movement is sometimes described as being synonymous with violence and Wahhabism, that is simply just not the case. Many Salafists consider the term Wahhabi derogatory. Wahhabism's explosive growth began, however, in the 1970s when Saudi charities started funding extremist Wahhabi schools (madrassas – see footnote 17) and mosques.

The overall Salafi movement can be divided into three groups – purists, activists, and jihadis – although the edges of these categories are blurred and, in fact, form a complex continuum from peaceful belief all the way through to violent terrorism. This is why despite some similarities, the different wings of contemporary Salafism are often strongly opposed to one another, even denying one another's Islamic credentials:

- Purists (or quietists) focus on preaching and education (avoiding political involvement as a diversion or even innovation (bida) that leads people away from true Islam.

- Activists also focus on political reform and re-establishing a caliphate through engagement and involvement in the civil sphere, but not violence. One of my friends, for instance, who works for a Christian theological college in the Middle East, has a good colleague who is a senior judge in the Sunni court in Saida (Sidon) and describes himself as a Salafi. He is also an inter-faith and peacemaking leader in Lebanon, a visiting lecturer at the Christian College, and has recently written a report on the need for non-violent approaches in post-conflict Syria.

- Jihadists, the third group, form a tiny (yet infamous) minority. They share similar political goals as the activists, but are committed to engaging in violence and terrorism to achieve them.

11 Bill Schwartz, *Islam: A Religion, A Culture, A Society*, Christians Aware, 2014, p.xviii.

For more read Meic Pearse, *Why the Rest Hates the West: Understanding the Roots of Global Rage*, Amazon, 2004.

12 *Discours de Paix* (Speech on Peace) Verdun. 20 July 1919.

13 'Carthaginian peace' is a term which derives from the imposition of the brutal 'peace' imposed on the city of Carthage by Rome, completely crushing it.

14 The Great Depression was a severe worldwide economic depression in the 1930s. The timing of the Great Depression varied across nations; however, in most countries it started in 1929 and lasted until the late 1930s. It was the longest, deepest, and most widespread financial crash of the 20th century.

15 The Gulf War (2nd August 1990 – 28th February 1991), code-named *Operation Desert Shield* (2nd August 1990 – 17th January 1991) for operations leading to the build-up of troops and the defense of Saudi Arabia and *Operation Desert Storm* (17th January 1991 – 28th February 1991) in its combat phase, was waged by coalition forces from 34 nations, led by the United States, against Iraq in response to Iraq's invasion and annexation of Kuwait.

16 The Sykes–Picot Agreement, formally known as the 'Asia Minor Agreement', was a secret agreement between the governments of the United Kingdom and France, with the assent of Russia, defining their proposed spheres of influence and control in the Middle East should they succeed in defeating the Ottoman Empire during World War I. The terms were negotiated by teams led by the French diplomat, François Georges-Picot, and soldier and Middle Eastern adviser to the British War Cabinet, Colonel Sir Mark Sykes. The negotiation of the treaty occurred between November 1915 and March 1916, and was

signed on 16th May 1916. It effectively divided the Arab provinces of the Ottoman Empire outside the Arabian Peninsula into areas of future British and French control or influence.

17 Madrassa is a term in popular usage across the broad spectrum of the various Muslim communities and schools of thought. Madrassa is derived from the Arabic word meaning 'a lesson', for which the plural is madaris in Arabic and madrassas in English. It is a huge sadness to most Islamic people that it has been hijacked in its contemporary usage by the popular media etc. I have a friend who, growing up in the UK, attended a madrassa on weekdays after school and on Saturday. She tells me that for her it was the name for 'after-school club', and was lots of fun, just like a club that a local church might run. It was great way to spend the holidays too.

In fact, madrassa denotes any type of educational institution, whether secular or religious (or of any religion). It derives from the Semitic root 'to learn, study' and, therefore, literally means 'a place where learning and studying take place'. The word has also entered various other Arabic-influenced languages such as: Urdu, Bengali, Hindi, Persian, Turkish, Azeri, Kurdish, Indonesian, Malay, and Bosnian/Croatian, with exactly the same innocuous meaning.

18 *We need to challenge the Jihadi narrative*, Tony Blair's speech on Tuesday, Oct 6, 2015, at the National 9/11 Memorial & Museum, New York, launching the *Inside the Jihadi Mind* report. Available from www.tonyblairoffice.org/news/entry/tony-blair-to-defeat-extremism-we-must-focus-on-the-religious-as-well-as-po/

19 Shiv Malik and Duncan Gardham. Tuesday, Oct 21st, 2014. www.theguardian.com/world/2014/oct/21/five-britons-week-travel-iraq-syria-isis

20 The Week, *What is Salafism and should we be worried by it?*

21 The Telegraph, Tuesday 18 Aug 2015, *What is the biggest threat facing the world today?* www.telegraph.co.uk/news/worldnews/big-question-kcl/11544853/What-is-the-biggest-threat-facing-the-world-today.html

22 Charlie Hebdo is a French satirical weekly newspaper that features cartoons, reports, polemics, and jokes. The cover of a 2011 issue featured a cartoon of Muhammad, whose depiction is forbidden in many interpretations of Islam. In 2012, the newspaper published a series of satirical cartoons of Muhammad, including nude caricatures. On 7th January 2015, two armed gunmen, brothers Saïd and Chérif Kouachi, forced their way into the magazine's offices in Paris. They killed 11 people and injured 11 others. After leaving, they also killed a French National Police officer outside the building. The gunmen identified themselves as belonging to Al-Qaeda.

23 Literary critic and philosopher Kenneth Burke first coined the expression 'scapegoat mechanism' in his books *Permanence and Change* (1935), and *A Grammar of Motives* (1945).

24 Girard contends that this is what happened in the narrative of Jesus of Nazareth. In his view, it is humankind, not God, who has need for various forms of atoning violence. Other well-known examples of scapegoating, for instance, include the vilification of the Jews in 1920s and '30s Germany, who were blamed for the German defeat in World War I, or of Sir Fred Goodwin the Chief Executive Officer of the Royal Bank of Scotland Group between 2001 and 2009, who came, in the popular mind, to symbolise the corruption of the banking sector and the UK's reckless overspending leading up to the 2007-8 crash.

25 www.firstlook.org/theintercept/2015/06/06/cia-director-john-bren-nan-admits-killing-people-countries-might-make-want-kill-us/

26 Published on July 10th, 2015. www.independent.co.uk/voices/letters/prevent-will-have-a-chilling-effect-on-open-debate-free-speech-and-political-dissent-10381491.html

27 Tony Blair concedes link between Islamic State and Iraq War. Oct 25th, 2015 www.bbc.co.uk/news/uk-politics-34630380/comments

28 The videotape was shown on Al Jazeera Television. www.youtube.com/watch?v=jHXLaio8G3I

29   www.firstlook.org/theintercept/2015/06/06/cia-director-john-bren-nan-admits-killing-people-countries-might-make-want-kill-us/

30   Rich O'Gorman & Andrew Silke, A. *Terrorism as Altruism: An Evolutionary Model For Understanding Terrorist Psychology.* In Taylor, M., Pease, K., & Roach, J., *Evolutionary Psychology and Terrorism: New perspectives on political violence.* Routledge. 2015.

31   Cameron's anti-terror strategy is *'barking up the wrong tree'*, says expert. Matthew Weaver, Monday July 20th, 2015. www.theguardian.com/uk-news/2015/jul/20/david-cameron-anti-terror-strategy-wrong-expert-says

32   *Woolwich attack: the terrorist's rant*, The Daily Telegraph. May 23rd, 2013.

33   Gregory of Nyssa (c. 335 – c. 395), also known as Gregory Nyssen, was bishop of Nyssa from 372 to 376 and from 378 until his death.

34   Dr. Martin Luther King, September 27th 1966. CBS Radio.

35   Dr. Martin Luther King, *The Other America* speech. Stanford University. April 14th, 1967.

36   In 2011, the UK government Department for International Development (DFID) defined globalisation as *'The process by which the world is becoming more and more connected and interdependent.'*

37   American support for Husni Mubarak over a 30-year period, for instance, whilst politically expedient, was viewed by many Egyptians as American complicity in oppression and corruption in direct opposition to the presentation of American values of Human Rights and Democratic principles.

Likewise, a 2004 the BBC claimed: *'During the anti-Soviet jihad Bin Laden and his fighters received American and Saudi funding. Some analysts believe Bin Laden himself had security training from the CIA.'* *Al-Qaeda's origins and links*, BBC News, July 20th, 2004.

Robin Cook, Foreign Secretary in the UK from 1997–2001, believed the CIA had provided arms to the Arab Mujahideen, including Osama bin Laden, writing: *'Bin Laden was, though, a product of a monumental miscalculation by Western security agencies. Throughout the '80s he was armed by the CIA and funded by the Saudis to wage jihad against the Russian occupation of Afghanistan.'* Robin Cook, The struggle against terrorism cannot be won by military means. Guardian Unlimited, Aug 7th, 2005.

38 www.theguardian.com/world/2015/dec/22/one-million-migrants-and-refugees-have-reached-europe-this-year-iom

39 Jonathan Swift, *Thoughts on Various Subjects*, 1711. Swift was an Irish essayist, novelist, & satirist.

40 Al-Azhar is an institution with a history stretching back over a thousand years and incorporates a mosque, a university and other educational institutions. The university has long been regarded as the foremost institution in the Islamic world for the study of Sunni theology and Sharia, or Islamic law. As its Grand Imam, Dr al-Tayeb holds a level of influence in Islam, not dissimilar to that of the Archbishop of Canterbury in Anglicanism.

41 Quoted by Andy Walton in *Archbishop of Canterbury and Grand Imam: We must work together to defeat ISIS*, Christian Today. June 10th, 2015. www.christiantoday.com/article/archbishop.of.canterbury.and.grand. imam.we.must.work.together.to.defeat.isis/55887.htm

42 *Grand Imam condemns Islamic State ideology and 'barbaric crimes'*, Mark Woods, Christianity Today, Dec 5th, 2014.

43 *Qur'*an or Koran? *Qur'*an is a more accurate transliteration of the Arabic word. Koran is the anglicised form. The word itself is Arabic and has letters that are not found in English – thus making a good phonetic translation difficult. The translation with a Q, however, is more accurate because the initial letter of the Arabic word is the Qaf which sound more like Q than K.

44 Muhammad lived from c. 570 CE – 8 June 632 CE. On his death, disagreement broke out over who should succeed him as leader of the Muslim community. None of Muhammad's sons had survived into adulthood, therefore direct hereditary succession was not an option. Umar ibn al-Khattab, a prominent friend of Muhammad, nominated Muhammad's father-in-law Abu Bakr. However, this choice was disputed by others, who held that Ali ibn Abi Talib, his son-in-law and cousin, had been explicitly named by Muhammad as his successor and therefore Muslim leadership belonged to him.

As a result Islam split into two separate groups:

Although the name took time to emerge, those who asserted Abu Bakr as first caliph were to become known as Sunnis. The term Sunni is derived from *sunnah in the term 'Ahl al-Sunnah wal Jamaah'*, literally, 'People of *Sunnah* (tradition) and community'. Hence Sunnis regard themselves as 'people of tradition (the tradition of the prophet) and community'.

Those who supported Ali ibn Abi Talibin as first caliph became known as Shias, which simply means 'the party of Ali'.

Although, in many places Sunnis and Shias have lived beside one another in peace, the rift has never been healed.

The great majority of Muslims are Sunnis – estimates suggest the figure is somewhere between 85 per cent and 90 per cent. Estimates of the number of Shia range from 120 to 170 million, roughly one-tenth of all Muslims.

In countries that have been governed by Sunnis, Shia tend to make up the poorest sections of society. They often see themselves as victims of discrimination and oppression. The opposite tends to be true in countries governed by Shia.

For instance, in 1979, the Iranian revolution launched a radical Shia Islamist agenda that was perceived as a challenge to conservative Sunni regimes, particularly in the Gulf.

In 1980, Iraq – led by Sunni leader, Saddam Hussein – invaded its neighbour, Iran, which was ruled by the country's Shia cleric, Ayatollah Khomeini. Saddam's goal was to replace Iran as the dominant state in the Persian Gulf. He was also worried that the Iranian revolution could have a ripple effect among his country's Shia majority.

The Bashar Assad regime in Syria, describes itself as secular; however, it is highly sectarian and its power base is in the Alawite community. Alawites are a minority Shia Islamic sect, centred in Syria. Alawites represent no more than 12 per cent of the Syrian population, but are also a significant minority in Turkey and northern Lebanon. The name 'Alawi' means followers of Ali. While the Shia community have been fighting for – or alongside – government forces, many young Sunni men have joined rebel groups.

In Lebanon: Hezbollah, literally 'Party of Allah', is a Shia Islamist militant group and political party. Hezbollah's paramilitary wing is the Jihad Council. Hezbollah was conceived by Muslim clerics, funded by the Shia regime in Iran following the Israeli invasion of Lebanon in 1982, and was primarily formed to offer resistance to the Israeli occupation. Its forces were trained and organised by a contingent of 1,500 Iranian Revolutionary Guards that arrived from Iran with permission from the Syrian government.

Britain has an estimated Muslim population of about 2.8 million. Of these around 5 per cent are Shia, the rest are Sunni.

45 Tony Blair's *We need to challenge the Jihadi narrative* speech. Tuesday, Oct 6th, 2015.

46 The *Centre on Religion & Geopolitics* has analysed a cross-section of 114 propaganda sources ranging from April 2013 to summer 2015 from three Salafi jihadi groups: ISIS, Jabhat al-Nusra, and al-Qaeda in the Arabian Peninsula. Its aim is to identify precisely which ideology is shared by the three groups, as revealed in their propaganda, in order to inform effective counter-narratives from mainstream Muslims, governments and civil society. Read the full report at www.tony-blairfaithfoundation.org/religion-geopolitics/reports-analysis/report/inside-jihadi-mind

47   www.bbc.co.uk/news/education-32977768

48   www.facebook.com/notes/the-archbishop-of-canterbury/
     we-must-confront-isil-as-part-of-a-global-response-to-religious-ex-
     tremism/919126308141516

49   It is not just adherents of religion that can act violently and oppres-
     sively toward others. The history of the 20th century is the record
     of atrocities, on a scale never seen before, of the barbarism of secular
     atheistic ideologies.

50   Dave Andrews, quoted by Dr. Craig Considine in a review of his book
     'The Jihad of Jesus: The Sacred Nonviolent Struggle for Justice' for The
     Huffington Post. Extracted from www.daveandrews.com.au/jihad-
     ofjesus.html

51   Farkhunda Malikzada was a 27-year-old Afghan woman who was
     lynched by a mob in Kabul on March 19th, 2015. Farkhunda was an
     observant Muslim who wore a veil (hijab). At the time of the attack,
     she had just finished a degree in religious studies and was preparing to
     take a teaching post.

     Farkhunda had been arguing with a mullah, named Zainuddin, in
     front of a mosque where she worked as a religious teacher, about his
     practice of selling charms at a religious shrine in Kabul. During this
     argument, Zainuddin reportedly accused her of burning the Qur'an.
     She responded, *"I am a Muslim, and Muslims do not burn the Qur'an!"*

     According to eyewitnesses, hundreds of angry civilians flocked to the
     mosque upon overhearing the mullah's accusation. They dragged out
     Farkhunda and started to beat her. She was thrown from a roof, run
     over by a car, and beaten with sticks and stones outside the mosque.
     The mob then set her body alight and dumped it in the Kabul River
     while police looked on. Farkhunda's parents said the killing was insti-
     gated by the mullah with whom Farkhunda had been talking, who
     began loudly accusing her of burning the Qur'an, *"in order to save his
     job and life."* An eyewitness said that the mob was chanting anti-Amer-
     ican and anti-democratic slogans whilst beating Farkhunda. Police
     investigations revealed that she had not burned anything.

52 An imam is an Islamic leadership position. The role is most commonly exercised in the context of leading a mosque and Muslim community by Sunni Muslims. In this context, imams may lead Islamic worship services, serve as community leaders, and provide religious guidance. However, for Shia Muslims, the term is far more specific and is often only applicable to those members of the house of the prophet ahl al-Bayt, designated as infallibles or as a title for renowned Muslim scholars.

53 Hadith are the collections of the reports claiming to quote what the prophet Muhammad said verbatim on any matter. The term comes from the Arabic meaning 'report', 'account' or 'narrative'. Hadiths are second only to the Qur'an in terms of their authority and seen as important tools for understanding it. They are based on spoken reports that were in circulation in society after the death of Muhammad, but unlike the Qur'an itself, were not compiled by a central authority. Hadith were evaluated and gathered into large collections during the 8th and 9th centuries, generations after the death of Muhammad, by various groups. Individual hadith are classified by Muslim clerics and jurists as sahih (authentic), hasan (good) or da'if (weak). However, there is no overall agreement: different groups and different individual scholars classify a hadith differently, added to which different branches of Islam (Sunni, Shia etc.) refer to different collections of hadith, whilst a small section rejects their authority altogether. Many elements of conservative Islam – such as the rejection of paintings, sculpture of living things and the stoning adulterers – are mentioned in hadith but not the Qur'an.

54 In Arabic, the word jihād is a noun meaning 'to strive, to apply oneself, to struggle, to persevere'. A person engaged in jihad is called a mujahid, the plural of which is mujahideen. The word jihad appears frequently in the Qur'an, often in the idiomatic expression 'striving in the way of God', to refer to the act of striving to serve the purposes of God. Although jihad is sometimes translated as 'Holy War', this is highly controversial. Many talk of jihad having two meanings: an inner spiritual struggle (the 'greater jihad'), and an outer physical struggle for Islam (the 'lesser jihad'), which for the vast majority of scholars must still be, of its very nature, non-violent.

55 Although the notion is somewhat underdeveloped in Islam, the term 'caliph' which is usually taken to mean 'successor' and thus to refer to the leader of a caliphate (a successor of Muhammad) can also mean 'steward':

'Caliph is a corruption of khalifah, which comes from the Arabic kahf, meaning to leave behind, and so a successor or vicegerent', writes M.J. Akbar. *'The Qur'an mentions two caliphs of Allah. The first was Adam, says the Qur'an (2:30) "Behold", thy Lord said to the angels, "I will create a vicegerent (khalifah) on earth." ... The second is David. "O David!" says verse 265 of surah 38, "We did indeed make thee a vicegerent on earth; so judge thou between men in truth (and justice)."'*

In this sense, the term 'caliph' becomes a declaration of Adam's and, through him, all humanity's role as God's vicegerent; the earthly representatives of the Divine.

56 For instance, the Vatican City's legislative authority is vested in the Pontifical Commission – a body of cardinals appointed by the Pope for five-year periods – but executive power remains in the hands of its President; the Bishop of Rome.

57 Sharia deals with an array of topics including crime, politics, marriage contracts, trade regulations, religious prescriptions, and economics, as well as sex, hygiene, diet, prayer, everyday etiquette, and fasting. For instance, Islamic banking (Sharia compliant finance) does not charge interest on loans, and investment in certain activities is prohibited. In the same way that there is not 'one Islam', there is also no 'one form' of Sharia law. Within the vast majority of Islamic thought, Sharia evolves and adapts over time, as it responds to different contexts and cultures.

58 From a TV address by President Barack Obama, from the Oval Office on Sunday night, Dec 7th, 2015, which discussed the mass shooting in San Bernardino, California, just a few days before.

59 Taken from the *The Concept of Bid'a in the Islamic Shari'a*. A lecture by Shaikh Nuh Ha Mim Keller at Nottingham and Trent University. Jan 25th, 1995. www.masud.co.uk/ISLAM/nuh/bida.htm

60 *Sunnah* literally means 'a clear or well-trodden path' and so has come to mean 'habit', 'custom' or 'tradition'.

61 There are four prominent approaches to fiqh within Sunni practice, and two others within Shia tradition. These schools are each named after the classical jurist (judge) who taught them. In Sunni practice Hanifite, Malikite, Shafite and Hambalite, and in Shia Islam Jafferite and Zaydist. Entirely separate from both the Sunni and Shia traditions, Khawarij Islam has evolved its own distinct school of Fiqh.

62 Reported by Martin Whittingham and Jenny Taylor. The Guardian. Friday May 28th, 2010. A mufti is an expert in Islamic law who studies the science of deriving practical legal rulings from the sources of Sharia such as the Qur'an and Hadith. They are qualified to give authoritative legal opinions – known as fatwas – around what is obligatory, recommended, permissible or prohibited.

63 These four values were first set out in the Prevent strategy of 2011. See https://www.gov.uk/government/publications/prevent-strategy-2011

64 *Tawhid*, also transliterated as *Tauheed* or *Tawheed*, is defined as the doctrine of God's unity or indivisible oneness. It is Islam's most fundamental concept.

65 *Ummah* is an Arabic word meaning 'nation' or 'community'. It is commonly used to mean the collective community of all Islamic peoples, bound together by ties of religion.

66 Özay Mehmet, *Islamic Identity and Development: Studies of the Islamic Periphery*, Routledge, 1990. p. 268.

67 Schwartz, p.xv.

68 This issue becomes a real problem for many non-western Christians. For instance, Andy Matheson, who has spent many years in India directing Oasis work there, often talks about the dichotomy that many Indian Christians find themselves in because their natural approach to life is communal, whereas the Church, heavily influenced by western writers and preachers, pushes them to aspire to think and behave in

a far more individualistic way (e.g. The 'Purpose Driven Life' type of approach to spirituality).

69   Schwartz. p.36.

70   Rashid Tahmina, *Secular State, Citizenship and the Matrix of Globalised Religious Identity*, Alternatives: Turkish Journal of International Relations, 6, no.1&2, 2007, p.158.

71   Schwartz, p.77-78.

72   The Qur'anic verse cited, most often, in this regard is: *'The punishment of those who wage war against God and His Apostle [Muhammad] and strive with might and main for mischief through the land is; execution, or crucifixion, or the cutting of hands and feet from opposite sides, or exile from the land; that is their disgrace in this world and a heavy punishment is theirs in the hereafter.'* (Qur'an 5:36).

73   Vincent J. Donovan, *Christianity Rediscovered: An Epistle from the Masai*. SCM Press. Second Edition. 1982. p.142.

74   Jurgen Moltmann, *God in Creation: A New Theology of Creation and the Spirit of God*, trans. Margaret Kohl, Harper & Row, 1985.

75   Early Saturday morning Nov 28th 2015.

76   www.theguardian.com/us-news/2015/nov/27/colorado-springs-shooting-planned-parenthood

77   Schwartz, p.xv.

78   Paul Hiebert, *Conversion, Culture and Cognitive Categories* in *Gospel in Context* 1:4 (Oct 1978), p. 24-29. Hiebert further discusses mathematical set concepts in his book *Anthropological Reflections on Missiological Issues*. Baker Books, 1994.

79   Breivik expresses his views in his 1,500-page book *2083 – A European Declaration of Independence,* which he published on the Internet on the same day as he committed the massacres. Quote via Massimo

Introvigne in *The Identity Ideology of Anders Breivik* www.cesnur.org/2011/mi-oslo-en.html

80   Rather than being one organisation, the modern day Klan is composed of a loose connection of small independent chapters across America. Experts estimate that there are presently something over one hundred different Klan groups around the country, with a combined strength of some 5,000 members and associates. Many chapters have formed strong alliances with other white supremacist groups, such as neo-Nazis, adopting the look and emblems of white power skinheads. The formation of independent chapters, however, has made Klan groups more difficult to infiltrate, and researchers find it hard to estimate their numbers accurately. It is believed that about two-thirds of Klan members are concentrated in the Southern United States, with the other third situated primarily in the lower Midwest. Source: *Ku Klux Klan – Affiliations – Extremism in America.*

81   Al-Khattar, Aref M, *Religion and terrorism: an interfaith perspective.* Westport, 2003, p.21, 30, 55, 91.

82   Michael Robert and Philip Rosen, *Dictionary of anti-semitism from the earliest times to the present.* Scarecrow Press, 1997, p.267.

83   Wyn Craig Wade, *The fiery cross: the Ku Klux Klan in America.* Oxford University Press, 1998. p.185. Wade's book traces the Klan from its beginnings after the American Civil War in Tennessee.

84   David Smith, 'Christian threats force Muslim convoy to turn back in CAR exodus'. The Guardian. 14th Feb 2014.

85   *Almost all mosques destroyed in Central African Republic unrest – The Times of India* Timesofindia.indiatimes.com. Mar 18th, 2015.

86   Bazile was a judge of the Caroline County Circuit Court, Virginia, His statement was part of his written judgement, dated Jan 6th, 1959. The Lovings eventually appealed their case to the US Supreme Court, which ruled in their favour on June 12th, 1967. www.encyclopediavirginia.org/opinion_of_judge_leon_m_bazile_january_22_1965

87   Popularly attributed to Shaw – the Irish playwright (1856-1959).

88   Pope John Paul II referred to Jews as *'our elder brothers and sisters in faith'*, whilst the present Pope explained that *'every Christian has Jewish roots.'*

89   Although the Bible says nothing of Abraham's early life, there is an old story that is still taught by Jewish rabbis around the world today. This story is found in the *Book of Jubilees* (an ancient – 150–100 BC – Jewish commentary on Genesis and part of Exodus, and considered part of the canon of the Bible by the Ethiopian Orthodox Church), and also referred to in the Qur'an (6:75–79).

The story explains that Abram's father, Terah, was an idol-maker in the city of Ur in Southern Mesopotamia (Modern-day Iraq). However, at an early age, his free-thinking son began to question the authenticity of all these idols. As far as he could see, logically, there could only be one God, not many.

As a young man, Abram eventually summoned the courage to confront Terah about all of this. One fateful day, he deliberately broke all his father's idols – except one – before calling his family and wider community to abandon their 'a local god for every occasion' approach to life and to choose instead a new commitment to seek and to worship the one true God; the God of everything and everyone.

But things backfired and, as a reward for this boldness, Abram found himself condemned by Nimrod, the king of Babylon, and thrown into a furnace. Miraculously, however, the fire failed to burn him and he escaped unharmed.

90   Muhammad was born and raised in the desert city of Mecca in Saudi Arabia. He was deeply spiritual, and from an early age would spend many hours alone in prayer. In his quest for the one true God he developed the habit of retreating to a cave on Mount Hira, three miles north of Mecca, for several weeks' seclusion, prayer and reflection each year.

It was there that, according to Islamic tradition, in the year 610, when he was 40 years old, in the month of Ramadan, while deep in contemplation, he was visited one night by the Angel Gabriel, who revealed to him some words, which now form part of the Qur'an (53:4–9). At first, he doubted the authenticity of the vision and had to be assured by others. Muhammad's first revelation was followed by others that continued until his death. He recorded the insights and words he was given, which eventually formed the text of the Qur'an.

Three years after his first revelation, Muhammad started preaching about what had been revealed to him. His simple, clear-cut message – that God is One, and that complete 'surrender' (literally islam) is the only way to discover God – drew huge crowds.

However, his popularity was seen as threatening to the Mecca authorities, and eventually he found himself driven from the city by its elders. As a result, in 622 he led his followers on a migration (Hijrah) to Medina. This journey was seen as so important that 622 became recognised as the beginning of the Islamic calendar. Within ten years, however, Muhammad had gained so many followers that he was able to return from Medina to Mecca. From here he continued to lead his community until his death in 632.

91 As Hebrew and Arabic are closely related Semitic languages, it is commonly accepted that Allah (root, ilāh) and the biblical Elohim are cognate derivations of same origin, as is Eloah, a Hebrew word which is used (e.g., in the Book of Job) to mean '(the) God.' Elohim and Eloah ultimately derive from the root El, 'strong', possibly genericised from El, the ancient Near Eastern creator god in pre-Abrahamic tradition. In Jewish scripture Elohim is used as a descriptive title for the God of the scriptures whose name is YHWH, as well as for pagan gods.

92 Fouad Elias Accad. *Building Bridges: Christianity and Islam.* Navpress, 1997. p.22.

93 Qur'an 29:46 (Translation Ali Quli Qara'i).

94 *'When God asked Jesus, son of Mary "Did you tell men to consider you and your mother as their gods besides God?" he replied, "Glory be to you! How could I say what I have no right to say? Had I ever said it, You would have certainly known about it. You know what is in my soul, but I do not*

know what is in Yours. It is You who has absolute knowledge of the unseen.'
Qur'an 5:116 (Translation Sarwar).

95 In fact, Volf draws on an unlikely ally in this, the 16th century German reformer monk Martin Luther, whom he shows argued that Muslims – like Jews, Catholics, and 'sectarian' Protestants – worship the right God, although he claimed they did it wrongly.

96 Perhaps the greatest insight that Volf offers is that, in the end, it is our *'practices [that] disclose the God (or the gods!) individual Christians or Muslims actually worship better than anything they or their holy book says about God's character or God's commands'.* Miroslav Volf. *Allah: A Christian Response*, HarperOne, 2011, p.115.

97 Schwartz, p.82.

98 Schwartz, p.82.

99 Schwartz, p.81.

100 Recognising the different concepts of revelation is, for instance, fundamental to a true understanding of how the two faiths differ from one another. Christians believe that in Jesus Christ the nature of God is revealed, and the way to a real – and personal – relationship with God is opened up. This idea is unthinkable to a Muslim for whom God is totally transcendent and wholly other. Instead, through the Qur'an, God has revealed the right way to live in society. The Christian looks for a saviour but, as Bill Schwartz puts it: *"The Muslim sees only the need of a guide …".*

101 Qur'an 49:13 (Translation Al-Hujurat).

102 Donovan. p.vii.

103 www.counterextremism.org/resources/details/id/68/learning-together-to-be-safe-a-toolkit-to-help-colleges-contribute-to-the-prevention-of-violent-extremism

104 The UK Government's overall approach to security and counter-terrorism is known as CONTEST. It is built around four areas of work:

- Pursue: to stop terrorist attacks

- Prevent: to stop people becoming terrorists or supporting terrorism

- Protect: to strengthen our protection against a terrorist attack

- Prepare: to mitigate the impact of a terrorist attack

    www.gov.uk/government/publications/2010-to-2015-government-policy-counter-terrorism/2010-to-2015-government-policy-counter-terrorism

105 Richard Rohr, *Falling Upward: A Spirituality for the Two Halves of Life*. Jossey-Bass. 2011.

106 Ivan Illich (1926–2002).

107 Steve Chalke, *Being Human*. Hodder & Stoughton, 2015. p.13.

108 www.army.mod.uk/join/ Extracted on 10th December 2015.

109 From the executive summary of *Dying to Belong: An In-depth Review of Street Gangs in Britain.* Available from The Centre for Social Justice, www.centreforsocialjustice.org.uk

    'More than 70 youngsters died at the hands of gangs in Britain in 2008, the year before the report was published. In London, 26 were stabbed to death. More than 170 gangs, with members as young as ten, have been identified by police in London alone. Many are loose affiliations of friends from the same area intent on controlling a 'turf' or territory, often defined by a postcode. The penalty for straying into the wrong area is to be robbed, beaten or stabbed. Many teenagers now routinely carry a knife out of fear, in order to defend themselves if attacked.'

    The UK Government has since adopted the definition of a street gang set out in the Centre for Social Justice's 2009 report:

'A relatively durable, predominantly street-based group of young people who:

1. see themselves (and are seen by others) as a discernible group;

2. engage in criminal activity and violence;

3. lay claim over territory (not necessarily geographical, but can include an illegal economy territory);

4. have some form of identifying structural feature;

5. are in conflict with other, similar, gangs.

110 www.bangkokpost.com/news/general/460424/teen-gang-throw-small-bombs-at-noodle-shop-kill-woman

111 www.standard.co.uk/news/crime/three-teens-convicted-of-murder-after-stabbing-church-ministers-son-and-leaving-him-to-die-in-street-10143963.html

112 www.ewn.co.za/2015/05/15/Manenberg-gang-violence-disrupts-schools

113 www.nydailynews.com/new-york/nyc-crime/died-hands-bronx-teen-mourns-bro-14-article-1.2233467

114 The *Youth gangs, knife and gun crime* bibliography is available from the Social Sciences Reference Service, The British Library, 96 Euston Road, London, NW1 2DB, United Kingdom.

115 Jessie Feinstein and Nia Imani Kuumba, *Working with gangs and young people: a toolkit for resolving group conflict.* Jessica Kingsley, 2006.

116 C. Strocka, *Youth gangs in Latin America.* SAIS Review of International Affairs, Vol.26, no.2, Summer-Fall 2006, p.133-14.

117 Kate Broadhurst, Head of Research with Perpetuity Research and Consultancy International (PRCI), University of Leicester. www.le.ac.

uk/ebulletin-archive/ebulletin/features/2000-2009/2006/08/nparticle.2006-08-03.html

118 *Dying to Belong*, Executive summary.

119 John Hagedorn, *A World of Gangs: Armed Young Men and Gangsta Culture,* University of Minnesota Press, 2008.

120 Ross Deuchar, *Gangs, Marginalised Youth and Social Capital,* Trentham Books Ltd, 2009.

121 Consider another growing world-wide issue, that of the educational underperformance of so many young people, especially boys, and especially boys from poor economic backgrounds, which recent years have also seen much research around. For instance, in 2012, UNICEF published *Why are Boys Under-performing in Education? Gender Analysis of Four Asia-Pacific Countries,* which looked at education in Malaysia, Mongolia, The Philippines and Thailand. www.unicef.org/eapro/report_why_are_boys_underperforming_FINAL.pdf

Clearly, there is no single reason why boys do poorly in school. However, the research is an analysis of the key factors – including economic, societal, and cultural issues – that cause the trend of poor performance. It also explores a variety of interrelated 'scholastic' factors including the learning environment, school response to limited budgets, language of instruction and academic streaming, the impact of transition, the lack of male teachers, learning styles and curriculum.

It goes on to identify various 'economic and social' factors which influence boys' underperformance, particularly low-income and migrant families, including government investment (which impacts the learning environment), family influences, customs and practices in socialisation, family involvement, and poverty and household economics.

122 Chalke. p.18. (Read my story in Chapter 1).

123 That is why, for instance, in maths, a radical sign ($\sqrt{}$), indicates the root of a number and why the radish (the root vegetable) is so named.

161

124 www.washingtonpost.com/news/acts-of-faith/wp/2015/12/05/
liberty-university-president-if-more-good-people-had-concealed-
guns-we-could-end-those-muslims/

125 This speech and scene is movingly recaptured as part of Richard
Attenborough's 1982 biographical film 'Gandhi'.

126 Augustine of Hippo, *Contra Faustum Manichaeum* Book 22, sections
69-76.

127 Based on Augustine's reading of Romans 13:4.

128 Matthew 5:44.

129 Judith Banister and Johnson Paige, *After the Nightmare: The Population
of Cambodia*. In *Genocide and Democracy in Cambodia: The Khmer
Rouge, the United Nations and the International Community*, ed. Ben
Kiernan, Yale University Southeast Asia Studies. New Haven, 1993.

130 Exodus 34:7, Numbers 14:18, Deuteronomy 5:9, Deuteronomy
24:16.

131 See Glen H. Stassen, *Just Peacemaking: Transforming Initiatives for
Justice and Peace*, 1992.

132 Matthew 26:52.

133 Dave Andrews, *The Jihad of Jesus: The Sacred Nonviolent Struggle for
Justice*. Wipf & Stock, 2015. p.26.

134 Some thoughts borrowed from an article by my friend Adam Philips.

135 Qur'an 33:7, Qur'an 42:13-14, Qur'an 57:26.

136 Qur'an 3:45. In fact, Jesus appears in 93 Qur'anic verses whilst
Abraham appears 69 times. Gregory A. Barker and Stephen E. Gregg,
Jesus Beyond Christianity: The Classic Texts, Oxford University Press,
2010, p.84.

137 A figure very similar to the Antichrist in Christianity.

138 There is no explicit reference to the al-Mahdi in the Qur'an, but references to him are found in Hadith, where, according to Islamic tradition, Isa will proclaim al-Mahdi as the Islamic community leader. Muslims believe that at that time Isa also will dispel Christian and Jewish claims about him.

139 Al-Shabaab, literally 'the Youth' or 'The Youngsters', is a jihadist terrorist group based in East Africa. It describes itself as waging jihad against 'enemies of Islam', and engaged in a holy war against the Somali government, its allies and supporters.

140 *UN Points to Progress in Battling Al-Shabab in Somalia* Jan 3, 2015. Retrieved 4 January 2015.

141 In June 2011, the UK Government launched a revised Prevent strategy, as part of its wider CONTEST, counter-terrorism strategy, aimed at stopping people from becoming terrorists or supporting terrorism. From September 2014, schools across the UK have been required to deliver against the Prevent strategy, with it now being fully integrated into the Ofsted inspection process.

Oasis is a ground-breaking global Christian movement and group of
charities and social enterprises working in 51 community hubs located in
11 countries across the world.

Oasis works with and within some of the most vulnerable communities, seeking
to become an integral part of every neighbourhood we work in. We achieve this
through the development of 'Oasis Hubs', which provide integrated services
designed to meet the breadth of human need. Our aim is to build communities
that are health, safe, supportive and full of opportunity; communities in which
every individual is supported to reach their God-given potential in life.

To find out more about Oasis in the UK visit **www.oasisuk.org**,
or for information about our global operations, visit **www.oasisglobal.org**

 @oasis_uk

 www.facebook.com/oasisuk

© Oasis Global
2016